The Singer Within
An Anthology of Poems

Kenneth G Robinson
Edited by Angela L Robinson

Published posthumously by

www.authorsonline.co.uk

An Authors OnLine Book

Copyright © Angela L Robinson 2008
Cover design © Richard Fitt

All Photographs copyright © Angela L Robinson

All rights reserved. No part of this publication may be reproduced, stored in a retrieval system, or transmitted in any form or by any means, electronic, mechanical, photocopy, recording or otherwise, without prior written permission of the copyright owner. Nor can it be circulated in any form of binding or cover other than that in which it is published and without similar condition including this condition being imposed on a subsequent purchaser.

The moral rights of the author have been asserted.

ISBN 978-0-7552-0434-2

Authors OnLine Ltd
19 The Cinques
Gamlingay, Sandy
Bedfordshire SG19 3NU
England

This book is also available in e-book format, details of which are available at www.authorsonline.co.uk

1917 - 2006

Kenneth Robinson

An Appreciation by Terry Waite CBE

Each Thursday evening in 1993 five or six people gathered to dine together in Trinity Hall Cambridge. Most were highly distinguished in their own fields of study and the conversation was invariably stimulating and frequently lasted until late in the night. Kenneth Robinson was a regular attender. He was of slight build and had an unassuming manner which did not betray a wealth of experience and intelligence, together with a depth of feeling and emotion now revealed in this lovely collection of his poetry. I knew Kenneth during the latter years of his life when we dined together. The frozen upper lip to which he refers (page 98) in his poignant poem 'The Generation Gap' rarely thawed in public but when, in the privacy of his own room, he took up his pen, he revealed an inner life that was rich and extended way beyond the bounds of his intellectual pursuits. He was a naturally modest man but in intellectual argument he was quite capable of producing the rapier and using it with deadly precision. However, the battle was never acrimonious and his poetry reveals the compassion that was an essential part of his character.

In his poetry Kenneth's intellectual and emotional life unite and we are the fortunate beneficiaries. 'One hope!' he writes in the poem Epitaph. 'Let me be eccentric'. Thank goodness he did not conform to type for this gentle man with a profound experience of all sorts and conditions has given us an insight into the source of his creativity. Here, in the depths of his inner life, pain and pleasure are reconciled as he gives us a glimpse of the harmony he so ardently desired.

Foreword by Laurie John

"Hail poetry, thou heaven-born maid!" So wrote W.S. Gilbert in the Pirates of Penzance. Many of his contemporaries turned their hand to verse, much of it of high quality. Indeed, the Victorian and Edwardian years witnessed an unprecedented outpouring of the art form that, incidentally, greatly enhanced our unique treasury of hymns by providing lyrics on religious themes. It is only when one travels to countries like France where this lyrical flowering did not take place and consequently there are virtually no hymns, that one realises how perceptive Gilbert was to hail our good fortune.

Kenneth Girdwood Robinson, 1917 – 2006, led a very full life indeed. Even at school, he cultivated an interest in China and the Chinese language and after a very active war, he returned to Oxford University to do a second degree with a focus on Chinese music. This brought him into contact with Professor Joseph Needham, who became a lifelong friend. This was followed by a career in Development Education in the Far East, later with UNESCO in Europe. In 1980 he was invited by Needham to join the Needham Research Institute in Cambridge where, until the very end of his life, he assisted in the editing, and indeed contributing to the monumental "Science and Civilisation in China". How did he find the time to write hundreds of poems and, more to the point, why did he write them?

Unlike our Victorian hymn-writers, Robinson had no strong religious convictions. However, like many of us, he was nevertheless a persistent seeker of "higher things". His guide in this quest was language. Robinson was a classicist steeped in Latin and Greek. He learned French, Japanese and Chinese and had more than nodding acquaintance with several other tongues. Words, for Robinson, not only had meanings, they each had a cloud of associations which profoundly enriched their capacity as vehicles for the transfer of ideas. The outcome, for him, could be an elevation to a universe of concepts that could almost be said to float above but nevertheless enfold the whole of reality. This perception chimed harmoniously with the Chinese philosophy of the Tao, to which he often felt drawn.

To put our feet of clay back on the ground, here, for example, is Robinson, in a footnote to a masterly little poem *"Second Youth"* (page 1), in which he comments on one line:

"Springs and summers, clouds and rain" reminds me that Chinese thinking is full of the idea that nature is both masculine and feminine. When heaven touches earth copulation takes place, designated by the rainbow. When a Chinese country girl saw a rainbow she would hide her face to shield herself from the consequences.

In private conversation, Robinson wondered whether such insights into the concepts that other cultures perceived in their language might not, given the chance, enrich our own. If so, this might be one good reason for welcoming the influx of immigrants that we were now witnessing.

Many a dramatist has set up a stage situation in order to explore what might happen under similar circumstances in real life. Robinson too, when emerging from a complex, sometimes disturbing experience, as during his wartime service, would often write a poem which mirrored that situation in order to make sense of it. See, for example *Thoughts of war in a Cotswold churchyard*, (page 115); and *Thoughts among the rubber trees*, (page 117)

Always fond of experimentation, he composed several poems in Basic English (on which he corresponded with its English progenitor, G.K. Ogden) with its restricted vocabulary of some 850 words. Far from producing attenuated verse, this discipline could produce clear shining gems such as *Gold and Silver*, (page 17). In this anthology the reader will also find poems playing with complex internal rhymes and sounds, poems with apt and suggestive layouts, as well as blank verse that pierces straight to the heart. I defy anyone to read *Generation Gap*, (page 98), and not be touched by:

"Early, much too early,
I was sent away to school,
Froze the upper lip
And learned to cry inwardly."

By contrast, one only has to read the masterpiece we have plucked out of context to begin this collection, *Second youth*, to find in Robinson a full-blooded connoisseur of life. Again, back at Oxford and well into his B.Litt. thesis he writes deliciously of a girl who caught his eye in the aptly titled *Restraint*, (page 16):

"I will have none of it, have none at all!
But if the cherry wantonly should fling
Her fragile beauty to the passers-by
For their delight, with racing pulse am I
To shut my door and write some Ode to Spring?"

If Robinson had been a writer who was simply energised and ignited by events, he would have emerged as yet another above-average poet. However, the stimulus in his case, occurring very strongly and often at inconvenient times, seems to zoom in from another dimension entirely.

"We would be just about to go out somewhere," he once told me, "when the hairs would stand up on my forearm and I would have to stop what I was doing, make everybody wait, quickly find pen and paper, and sit down and write!" The Greeks used to speak of being "touched by the finger of the muse" and in a beautifully crafted note to *Slow Beat*, (page 89), Robinson speaks of a poem "pouring itself onto the page". It is almost as if the poet becomes the channel for a richly creative stream whose source is utterly outside him. While this is happening Robinson says he is conscious of "a terrific interplay of words, so many that when the writing is done many of them evaporate and many of the secondary meanings disappear."

In the course of our conversations, during which my friend asked whether I would be willing to edit his poems for posthumous publication, I suggested that he wrote notes to give the background to as many of them as were appropriate. This he duly did and these notes add an extra depth and can be startlingly informative. (If you would like to know how the Arabs copied the idea of the magic carpet from the Chinese but got it all wrong, read on!) In the note to *Slow Beat*, he manages to "kiss the joy as it flies" and the result is a revealing and beautiful snapshot of what it is like to be touched by the muse's finger.

He takes for example the penultimate verse:

"Together we had merriment
  Till candles guttered, and no less
Beneath the crumbling pediment
  The graces bless
Others like us...."

"I myself have had joyful days with my loved woman, ignoring time till reminded by the guttering of the candles. Now I realise that time has been passing, that whole civilisations have perished, but even after a civilisation has gone, a graciousness lingers, which blesses those people who are aware of it."

Now, like the civilisations he refers to, Kenneth Girdwood Robinson has, alas, perished. His highly valued and well-loved presence is gone. But summoned by his poetic legacy, a graciousness does indeed linger. An enriching graciousness by which the reader is eternally blessed, and grateful.

Laurie John

Acknowledgements

Special thanks to our friend of many years, Laurie John who, in writing such a splendid foreword, has paid great tribute to Kenneth. Laurie's help both in sorting the poems and in many other ways was invaluable. And to our many friends and large family for the love, support and encouragement in a book I know Ken would be proud of, a big thank you from us both.

Also a large thank you to Terry Waite for his kind appreciation, and to James for all the early crucial work he and Delia put in.

Angela Robinson.

All comments following poems are those of Kenneth Robinson with the exception of those marked:

LHJ - Laurie John

AR - Angela Robinson

Contents

Second Youth

When these hot fires within me have died down,
And propped on cushions I survey the dark,
What phantom faces will obsess my brain?
Shall I, by cold hearth clamped, await one spark
Which will leap up and float like thistledown,
Recalling in its instant's transient glory
Long vanished springs and summers, clouds and rain?
Will that small point redden and redden yet
Till poppies, roses, brave carnations bloom
And dancing days return, cheeks glow, lips wet
From many kisses plead for more? That story,
Will it again unfold? Will they forget
If I remember, I, who break their tomb
And summon my loves to join me and dance at the day of
doom?

31 July 1947

*Written very quickly, before leaving Rollright for
Oxford. "Springs and summers, clouds and rain"
reminds me that Chinese thinking is full of the
idea that nature is both masculine and feminine.
When heaven touches earth copulation takes place,
designated by the rainbow. When a Chinese
country-girl saw a rainbow she would hide her
face.*

1

Requiem for Myself

Some year in future loam, men will discover
my town and citadel of bone, but never
know how it teemed and whispered myriad songs.

"Here" they will say, "within this empty dome
sat old King Crafty, framing all day long
rationalisations for his inexcusable actions …

Here in this hollow chamber, orator Tongue
echoed his master; there through unwinding ways
poured in the murmur of the day's transactions.

Through these two apertures, like honeycomb
when honey is no more, nor any bees,
filtered the odours of that early day,

While from twin spy-holes, scanning the shifting seas
of faces that he knew – foe, traitor, lover,
he queried the mad polity where he made one".

Yet I was not polite. I was alone,
and one, in one brief instant's lost perfume.
Here is my history, long fled away ….

Sunset

Slowly the sun drops, burning the poplars;
    And those straight sentinels of day stand grim and still,
Staring bewildered, as over a blazing kingdom.

Glorious day is over. Sunk is an empire.
    Shattered the brazen legions that trampled the
shadows,
And now in flight they swiftly steal away.

Heralds the night! Dusk summons him long and coldly.
    Swarthy his shadows gathering over the plain
Sweep all before them into the rim of sunset.

Lower the crimson standard dips – and is gone.
    Rank upon rank the riotous stars surge forth
Wheeling in numberless squadrons over the darkness.

Now you may sleep, sentinels; sleep in the gardens.
    Here roses once dreamed in the evening, and shadows
        now whisper,
Calling forlorn for the light, but the day is entombed.

10 October 1933

*Written when Kenneth was 16, this is an example of
many of the poems he wrote from the age of 8 which
are too numerous to be included in full. AR.*

Loneliness

Long shadows stretch across the grass
And cling to one that must depart;
And all is still and poppy-numbed,
Clasped in the red day's last embrace.
    Now every leaf half swooning hangs
And sees the warm sun drawn from sight,
Leaving but sorrow and remorse
For high hopes faded, brave desires
Grown strangely silent, golden days
Now shadowed by the gathering years:
But still there linger fainter things
That hover half remembered yet,
Where roses cloud the evening air –
Long, long ago, and deep delight.
    And then despair and endless pain
    Call for an everlasting night.

1934

*Written on a University College, Oxford post card -
but as Kenneth was just 16 at the time, perhaps he
was paying a preliminary visit. AR*

Twilight in Rome

Soft through the dim street drifts a murmur
   Lisping of roses and wine and jest.
The bright-lit houses of pleasure re-echo
   Donec virenti canities abest.

Now in the low-moon hour of twilight
   Snowy white shoulders gleam at their best,
And myrrhy hair falls rich with spangles
   Donec virenti canities abest.

Does not the face of a lovely woman
   Mock the red rose on a rose-white breast ?
Is not the warm sweet night for dancing
   Donec virenti canities abest ?

Music dies, and joy is gone by morning.
   Swift melts the hour by lovely lips caressed.
Then banish sleep, nor welcome day's returning
   Donec virenti canities abest.

Beauty fades as a brief night passes.
   Pale petals droop on the lingering guest.
Come then, fill up those sparkling glasses
   Donec virenti canities abest.

18 Feb 1935

See the comments on 'Twilight in Rome' on the next page.

Comments on 'Twilight in Rome'

Written at school (Wrekin, Shropshire) on 18 February 1935. My English teacher told my parents he thought I must be sexually precocious, but in fact this poem was entirely derivative from the book by Walter Pater - Marius The Epicurean. In April I went to live with a family in France near St. Gaudens in the Pyrenees. There were no young people there, and my professor, Mons. Emil Coulon de Pimentel, was afraid I should acquire a strong meridional French accent if I consorted with the young people of the village. However, he steered me safely through all the Drames of Racine. I emerged after six months in France speaking with the fastidious regard for the correct use of the subjunctive of a French professor.   In October I entered University College, Oxford.

Twilight in Provence

> Now is the hour when the sounds of day
>   Vanish away in the night.
> Only the peasants faint "a-aah"
> From the fields afar to his laden team
> Belong to the light.
> The crickets shrill from valley to hill
>   In their multitudes. By the stream
> The thin gold bell of the toad in the weeds
>   Echoes ringing above,
> And the loud frog shouts to the night his love,
>   His love, his love, in the reeds.

August 1936

I was living with Mons. Emil Coulon de Pimentel in the village of Riviere, a few miles from Saint Gaudens in Haute. Garonne. It was not a good place to learn French as everyone spoke it in a broad meridional accent, (Le chienng mange du painng etc.) but I emerged in September having read all the plays of Racine and with a heightened appreciation of Shakespeare.

In those days the night was full of sound. The peasants shouted at the cows, and occasionally oxen, which dragged the lighter loads. The stream was packed with frogs keeping up their nightlong brekkikekex, koax, koax, and the toads had a special musical tinkle known locally as the cloche d'or. When we went there a few years ago I was saddened to find that all the once familiar sounds had disappeared, or had been replaced, for example, oxen by tractors.

Crisis

Listen to the throbbing of the fever drums.
My head in sweaty pillow plunged, I hear
My inward pulse beat with the life of ocean.
Rocked amid the spindrift never comes
Tomorrow's father-threat. Relaxed I lie
Like a little child under a cloudless sky,
Content with all-sufficing mother-motion.

Motion that bred my struggle out to light !
Horror of dark, fear of the winding tunnel,
Gasp of cold air -- and now this thing is done;
Now fever drums summon me through the night,
Killing of goats with knives, their bleeding,
crying,
All this is mine ! My other selves are dying.
I in disintegration now am one !

26 Nov. 1946

This poem was published in the Oxford University magazine Isis. I had only just returned from the "Far East", bringing apparently some disease with me, for on the night of 26 November I dreamt of falling into some deep hole from which I could not escape, and on waking my heart was pounding furiously. When sufficiently recovered I wrote this poem.

Infant Rage

Before I learned this clumsy speech
  or clogged my limbs to make them walk
  I with my wordless golden talk
strode to the hills the stars to reach.

Swift as a falling star I plumbed
  the malachite bottom of the lake.
  Under the thundering cataract
to water's music I succumbed.

Floating on high when day was gone
  I saw the candles shine below.
      Warm air and cold would softly blow,
Silver and blue the broad sea shone.

Distance was not, and time stood still.
  The scent and colour of each flower
  Burned into song and danced. I yet
tremble that dancing to distil ---

Distil in words of clay to make
  A pattern on a printed page!"
  A voice I hear of infant rage
Bid me the lying mirror break.

8 February 1947

See the comments on 'Infant Rage' on the next page.

9

Comments on 'Infant Rage'

This poem attempts to bring to life some of the impressions one had when very young. When children sing, for example, it does not need to mean or say anything comprehensible to adults. The same is true of their early paintings.

Planting a Tree

(For James Ivar, my son).

Little one, did we put you in cold earth,
You, whose small body I'd had in my arms,
A warm weight for a time, with fingers gripping?
　　　You were a fire come like a star from space,
And like a star, gone to the dark places.
The earth our mother will make us new faces,
But will never again make us your face.
The red flowers went from view in the hollow,
Went from view like a flame burning my heart,
And now in the quiet you are, and quiet will be …
　　　But when the Spring comes, and all the earth is
talking
Of bees and winds and work, you will have your part
With the wine blood of the flowering almond tree.

26 February 1942

*My son James Ivar died on 8th February 1942 aged
only 8 weeks. He was buried in the churchyard of
Great Rollright, Oxfordshire. Putting a person in
to the cold receiving earth seems a callous thing to
do, but Robert Louis Stephenson, writing to a friend
the day after the funeral of his mother, said: "We
put her to earth yesterday." The tree which we
planted by his grave was an almond and lasted
almost 50 years. Angela and I replaced it in 1992.*

Love

I love thee and I love thee!

Thou with the crimson lips, the burning flower,

Now and I take thee in thy magic hour,

Now thou art mine tho' all time slips

To it's dark abyss.

      Great waterfalls unending

Surge and boil about me. Ours the blending

Of hope and perfume, softness and strongness.
Thou

A little blossom dangled on a bough,

A petal broken on the wing past mending.

Oh, that the ending were tomb's rending now.

26 May 1943

This was the only time I used "Thous" and "Thees".

12

Not Again

Turning the pages of my best book over
I saw a folded paper there;
And then you came like spring upon me,
You of old, like spring, and smiling;
You by the water's edge in summer,
Or when the early leaves are falling,
Ranging the fields and mists of morning.
You, who went, and softly laughing
Took away my everything.

Take them all, and keep them, laughing.
Take my heart and take my verses;
Take it all, but not the Spring.

Undated, but an early poem. L.H.J.

13

Requiem

Now it is near the time of falling apples.
Through meadow mist comes up an orange moon
Whose light ungilds our honey-stone, and dapples
The church's windows. Through this heavy door
We came together -- (sweet are promised apples) --
When France was falling on a brilliant afternoon,
And England's vivid summer lay before.

       Yet rang their thunder through our open door,
A whirlwind roaring . . . . . poverty or wealth . . .
Eastward and West . . . .in sickness or in health . . .
Towards no certain cross, beyond what shore?
Now thunders ebb, and roses flame again,
While gay days dance and delicately tiptoe over death.
Let Earth receive as Heaven engenders breath,
And Spring with a flash of almond banish pain.

28 November 1945

Written in Singapore

My Woman

This is my woman. Call her wife?
I care not what the priests have said.
Woman she is. Her breath and life
Are more to me than wedded bed.

We have seen suns and stars with eyes
Which might have never seen before.
Together phantom worlds arise;
Asunder I can dream no more.

When time and space we reconcile
And once again together stand,
We shall reign over that lost isle
Which was our land.

26 Feb. 1946

*Compare with Villanelle for Angela (p23), written
nearly half a century later. L.H.J.*

15

Restraint

When snow lay soft as wool beneath my feet
A dainty girl came gaily down our street.
A thousand diamonds sparkled on her hair.
Coldness I can endure when passing fair.

When fields are stripped and trees shake crooked
fingers,
When proper folk put pumpkins in the church,
Why out of doors my reputation smirch
Because one lover of the wan moon lingers?

When sun is hot, and cuckoo cannot call,
When shade entices by the ferny wall
And grass is lush, your lovely body keep;
I will have none of it, have none at all!

But if the cherry wantonly should fling
Her fragile beauty to the passers-by
For their delight, with racing pulse am I
To shut my door and write some Ode to Spring?

4 May 1947

University College, Oxford.

Gold and Silver

I and my money
    Are quickly parted,
    But happy-hearted
      I'd have it so.
Gold without measure
    Is mine for taking,
    My love's hair making
      Our troubles go.

When it is winter
    And winds are colder,
    When we are older
      And have no gold
Your hair of silver
    Will be my making,
    Ever awaking
      The days of old.

1948

This poem uses only the Basic English vocabulary of 850 words. It was accepted by the editor of Oxford Poetry, who said it was the best poem he had received that year. The poem refers to the noted golden hair colour of KGR's wife Peggy. A.R.

Villanelle

Lovely maidens have I known,
    Coral lips and dancing eyes.
Let us reap as we have sown.

Ere the summer rose is blown
    Why be prematurely wise?
Lovely maidens have I known.

Girls there are with hearts of stone.
    They shall thus philosophize:
Let us reap as we have sown.

Winter finds us all alone.
    Do not now the Spring despise.
Lovely maidens have I known.

Soon our dancing days are flown.
    All may then be spite and lies.
Lovely maidens have I known:
Let us reap as we have sown.

*I seem to have no record of when this was written.
At a guess I would say soon after the war, perhaps
1948. It was deliberately contrived to get
experience in the form of the villanelle, and to
make sure that the first and third lines can bear
repetition.*

18

Love's End

Nicolette, now evening is all about us
green and black, your hair with a thousand fine strands
trawls me deep. Most gladly I hear the call, and
    swim to the feasting.

Nicolette, your hair ripples like a dark wave
over pale sand breaking before the day break.
I, a drowned man, lie in the depths imploring
    your benediction.

Nicolette, your hair is a noose to hang me,
or a winding sheet to be wound around me.
Blest the man that may never more escape this
    myrrhy entombment.

30 June 1973

*Written in Buea, Cameroon, using the metre
developed by SAPPHO - phinetai moi keinos isos
theo isin, or in Catullus' Latin translation, Ille mi
par esse deo videtur.*

Commemoration Ball

You had little shoes --
Starry - toed they twinkled well.
Dance - how they danced with the grey dawn
breaking.
Now, when I think of it, my heart stops aching.
You and I, we lasted well.
Where are now those little shoes?

You had red lips
Soft and deep as peonies,
God - how we kissed till the green dawn caught us.
Those were the great days; mad love taught us
That sunrise and peonies
Were paler than your red lips.

Then there was music
Throbbing on the garden air,
All those melodies no-one ever sings now.
Songs like sunlight flashing on a bronze prow
Tell me that Pan lives, time is flooding back, and now
Spills on the garden air
His antique music.

1 May 1974

Written thirty-five years after University College,
Oxford, held their last Commem. Ball, before the
Second World War put a stop to such light-hearted
nonsense! The girl I was dancing with, (Peggy
Harvey), became my wife in the following June,
eleven days after I had waded to liberty from the
beach at Dunkirk with my wedding trousers round
my neck, the surface of the sea being thick with oil!
The song Jeepers Creepers reminds me of the days
when youth could deal with disasters!

Terminus

We met upon a road in the hot south,
Pole star distant, golden fruit
   the planets; then with hand and mouth
traced the never-repeated story to its root.
   Scarcely I noticed that the end was clear
as fading sunset, melting snow
music like surf swept up and, gathering slow,
   sparkled an everlasting instant.
                Dear
   dear love, now must I listen, now must hear
that other music like the dark Rhine flowing
   beyond the terminus of our delight.
Can insubstantial words describe our going
   or bid farewell while you are warm and near?
   Now must I face the dark, the bitter night.

Hamburg 1979

Relates to December in Cologne.

Goodnight My Love

I miss my love most sadly.
   Her eyes are hazel bright.
   When wishing her goodnight
I would have stayed most gladly.
I would have stayed in places
   Where there is no departing,
No greeting alien faces;
     But meeting tells of parting
       And I must say goodnight.

1992

In the autumn of 1992 Angela went down to Aldeburgh to take care of elderly friends. I was only able to join her at weekends as I was working in Cambridge. Our life seemed to be full of partings at that time. This little poem might be grouped or contrasted with Fortune of Soldiers, *(page 76).*

Villanelle for Angela

Your world, our world, may through all space extend,
    And we may wander past the Milky Way.
Then let us love till Time is at an end.

Morning and night with joy and sorrow blend,
    And all tomorrows make one yesterday.
Your world, our world, may through all space extend.

Though little sorrows never wholly mend,
    Griefs tall as mountains crumble into clay.
Then let us love till Time is at an end.

You would I gladly hold, and you defend
    Till none remains to challenge or dismay.
Your world, our world, may through all space extend.

Extend forever; smiles renew, lips send
    Eternal ripples on their endless way.
Then let us love till Time is at an end.

Though end all finite things, stars burst, cliffs rend,
    We shall go on in joy, your singing gay.
Your world, our world, may through all space extend.
Then let us love till Time is at an end.

19 March 2001

See the comments on 'Villanelle for Angela' on the next page.

23

Comments on 'Villanelle for Angela'

"Is no one inspired by our present picture of the universe? The value of science remains unsung by singers. You are reduced to hearing not a song or a poem, but an evening lecture about it. This is not yet a scientific age". Richard P. Feynman in What do you care what other people think ?

Aequanimitas

Sunlight is falling on the solid wall;
The curtain fidgets in a light wind.

Dandelions lose their feathered heads,
But the meadow waits for night relaxed.

Though little branches may never be still
Trees on the skyline keep their dignity.

Why should I be ruffled by this and that
When the wind-whipped clouds themselves sail on serene?

16 September 1944

An early experiment at reproducing the parallelism of Chinese poetry   Sunlight/curtain. Falling/fidgets. Solid/light. Wall/wind etc. To begin to get the feel of a Chinese poem the lines would have to rhyme. In addition Chinese poems often follow the tonal movements of a tune. Onomatopoeia is possible in the sound of the words, but also the written characters have their own onomatopoeia with for example a cluster of characters using the symbol for water if the poem is about lakes, rivers or rain.

Aequanimitas is the personal quality of calmly accepting whatever comes in life.

Rhymes To Measure

I have no time for this very scientific precision

Which holds up the lines of the poet to derision

and takes his lovelier thought and vision for elementary mistakes!

I am utterly tired of division and multiplication of what is or seen

I must insist on dreams!

17 April 1947

An early attempt at a vowel tune and internal rhymes - precision, derision, vision, division.

26

Easter Sacrifice

Seamless the sky, unraining yet !

Music again I hear. Without regret

I clasp my pain, stab discords. Mortal fret

Sees drought and flood corrode my brain.

Let me its waves forget, which sap and drain

Blood after sweat, for on the plain here, I

In dread must greet our pharmacy of slain

From whose dry eyes, behold ! our land is wet.

20 April 1949

See comments on 'Easter Sacrifice' on the next page.

Comment on 'Easter Sacrifice'

I was back at Oxford and well into my B.Litt thesis. Contributing to it was the work I had done for Joseph Needham on acoustics in China, which became a section of his Science and Civilisation in China, Vol IV, part 1. In studying early forms of music I found that a musical element was creeping into my poetry, consisting of a few selected vowels. Vowels themselves consist of two or more frequencies combined. The ancient Egyptians used to chant vowel hymns to the planets. This musical vowel element in poetry quite often occurs unconsciously, but I did not meet anybody who explored it deliberately. In this poem I was concerned with two vowels only:- the short [e] and the long [ei], as in raining yet; again regret; pain fret; waves forget, and so on. A more complex example of this vowel music will be found in Forsaken Music, on the next page.

I was moved to write Easter Sacrifice when I learnt that our word pharmacy is of Greek origin for in early times when the primitive races were afflicted by lack of rain the method of dealing with the drought was to bind one or more men up in hides, and put them in the sun. Thirst and the drying and contracting of the hides caused terrible suffering to the dedicated men, and it was felt that the gods responsible for the coming of the rain must surely take pity on them. In Greek they were called pharmakoi, "medicine men".

Forsaken Music

In the city Noise is lord. Birds are muted;
bells hum unheard in airy steeples
blurting rejected moments. The people press
and surge to a goal of steel which none dispute.
But in my restless fever a fluting stirs
and I yearn for redress, and shake to a wild music
which still in the soul burns, banishes pain,
and turns me again to the temple steps, where of old
a thousand throats echoed the planet's murmur,
and slow chanting healed the world's confusion.

11 Nov 1950

*This was the second poem which experimented with
a musical pattern composed of vowel sounds. (See
Easter Sacrifice, on the previous page). In my case
it was written very quickly, and the musical pattern
identified later. It consists of four vowels - ɔ: which
occurs ten times, tolling in each case like a great
bell, (though bells were unknown in Ancient Egypt
and in the Roman Empire before the age of the
Antonines; by which time the knowledge of the
magnificent bells of China are beginning to
spread). The vowel which tolls its way through
Forsaken Music is the ɔ: as follows line by line.*

Myself

I came into a land of fire and stone;
   No living trees were there, and nothing green,
But only stone and fire, and broken bone,
   Brown teeth of horses, and dead men were seen.
High over that long waste of burning sand
   Great birds, black-winged, were wheeling in the sky.
   Still I went on and on . . . . . But was it I,
That walker in a strange and wasted land?
But was it I, or someone new to me,
Who takes me with him, whom I never see?

A poem in Basic English, from the period when I was experimenting to see how much atmosphere one could develop with a limited vocabulary.

30

Capricorn and Cancer

Winter. Still the palms droop listless by the listless seas.
The same huge moon sits fat upon the waters; fishermen's lights
Flicker-burn in boats scarce rocked by ripples. These tropic nights
Flush to no May bloom, drink no gold September,
shrill to no mad March breeze.

> Far away we sense
> The shrinking
> Day;
> The world's cold shoulder
> Turned to the Pole
> Star.

Now come snipe, whipping Siberia's chill air and vast;
"Autumn's reached China at last" proclaim chestnuts sold in
our street.
These echoes of seasons reluctantly die. Though I love
humid heat
I know the first breath of the violet can only succeed
winter's blast.

10 December 1953

*I had had one year in Singapore and Malaya in
the army after the war. This was written after my
first year in Singapore following a career in the
East. This is an early example of the poems I wrote
later, playing with the idea of shaping the poem
physically.*

Fin de Siècle

New troubles come upon me fast,

    The green grass withers, brown leaves fall,

        And fails the day as hope is dying

    I hear no sound, no voice replying.

Every rose must droop at last.

    I have seen palaces and splendours,

        The red and gold where banners fall.

    New troubles come upon me fast.

    Rich cities burn where kings surrender.

    Chokes in tears the nightingale;

    And fails the day as hope is dying.

    No nightingale is heard replying.

        Every rose must droop at last.

Now troubles come upon me fast

    Around are endless armies crying,

    And fails the day as hope is dying.

        Every rose must droop at last.

11 November 1970

The Tao of Things

Now
tall
cypress
by whose root
at break of day doves
peck , peacocks strut and spread,
here
my last fruit is
dropped, shed.
Here have I
bled.
Yet
still
spurting, sap from the root
from the root sap springs up. I   would
not sip dew   .
from a frozen cup, nor kiss
worm in lip, but fire and snow renew
spent
corn.
All
earth, all seasons, all proclaim me one in time perpetual

13 November 1989

See comments on 'The Tao of Things' on the next page.

33

Comments on 'The Tao of Things'

We were in Ireland staying at Whites in Wexford
where in the evening we enjoyed the opera. Whites
has a reputation for treating all its guests as
members of a house party, and a very good
atmosphere develops. When about to go to bed at
midnight I felt an urge to write something. But
what? Then I remembered that some of the late
Roman poets had amused themselves and their
friends by writing poems in the shape of objects such
as a pot or jug or a tree. I decided to write one in
the shape of a cypress tree. What is the Tao, the
nature of a cypress? Certainly very different from
an oak or a poplar. This poem first saw the light
not as a cypress with wide-spreading branches, but
rather as an hourglass. Immediately new words
begin to cluster as the sands of time begin to fall,
from the upper bulb -- heaven -- to the lower one,
earth, or hell? It is a long time since the Romans
wrote such poems, but the human mind today is
much the same.

Magic Carpet

Behold! My Arabian carpet is red.
But see how the thread of Bokhara sky-blue
Is led into view, interwoven with green
Till the true dye is seen at the foot and the head,
Woven clean like a bed of fresh roses in dew
Which are wed to the hue of the rose that has been.

On a camel, the fleetest of beasts you may go.
You may travel till night. Even so I shall be
Long ago at my ease. You shall see me recline
With three women pouring my wine chilled with
snow
As I dine, saying "Lo, bring my carpet to me.
To and fro did we flee. Magic thing, thou art mine."

This began as an experiment with internal rhymes resembling the patterns in weaving. It went on to selected vowel melodies within the verse.

Magic carpets began in China. A Taoist expert beginning the training of a novice would sit with him on a carpet. In time they would be able to separate their minds from their bodies and to look down on themselves from above. Gradually the height would be increased till they were looking at their carpet far below in the palace grounds. Then they would start space travelling. The Arabs took this idea up, but mistakenly imagined that the magic was in the carpet and not in the minds of the practitioners! (Cont.)

KR's note, on the arrangement of rhymes-

	thread	Red
		blue
led	view	green
true	seen	head
clean	bed	dew
wed	hue	been

		go
	so	be
ago	see	recline
three	wine	snow
dine	lo	me
fro	flee	mine

36

Separation

I call to you among the hills,
    Where high snows peer through broken cloud.
        But never comes your voice replying.
        I hear no echoes slowly dying.
My heart with frosty silence fills.
        Between us huge Saharas burning.
    Wither the thoughts that to you crowd.
I call to you among the hills.
      You to my thoughts return, and turning
    Strike from my heart a shower of stars,
        But never comes your voice replying.
        I hear no echoes slowly dying.
My heart with frosty silence fills,
        When twilight dims and greys to starlight
I call to you among the hills
        "Jeanette-anette-anetta" crying.
        But never comes your voice replying.
My ear with frosty silence fills.

Alignment of lines by rhymes.

Hazy Spring

This hazy spring I hear a pigeon hail
First light in the morning leaves, and laugh
For joy of buds on glossy branches born.
I yet another summer now will see
The dainty apple dandled, or delight
In glowing cherries, baskets crammed with coals
Burning below me in the beetle grass.
Swifter and swifter like the winds that pass
Races each summer, and inexorably rolls
Each winter on, nor halts nor stands the Night;
But thick clouds gather, thunders threaten me,
Dark waters fall, fields fallow, skies are torn,
Storms rend us, and our friends are gone like chaff
Vanished forever from the lashing flail.

11 April 1950

Comments on 'Hazy Spring'

Written when living at Oxford and in London in order to complete my contribution to Needham's _Science and Civilisation in China,_ and my B. Litt. thesis on Equal Temperament in China. This verse form had been developing out of the sonnet. I called them "fish-tailed sonnets." In orthodox sonnets there is a break in the mood and rhyming of the poem after the eighth line. It may be traced back to the troubadours. But the troubadours apparently learnt it from the Arabs. If I may be bold to speculate the Arabs learnt it along with much useful arithmetic including the decimal placing of numbers from right to left, as in 2, 32, 432, which had been the Chinese system for grouping numbers in tens, for two thousand years. The solemn state hymns used in ceremonies also were constructed on the principle that there must be a change of mood indicated by a change of musical "mode" at least once per hymn. If this verse form was learnt from the Chinese by the Arabs and transmitted to the West it would explain why our earlier sonnets have a distinct change of mood after the eighth line.

The Everlasting Dance

Tossed in the turmoil of tempestuous chance
  like children chasing rainbow phantoms ever,
    we down this shifting life see dreams go drifting,
      grasp them, gasp and despair at mirage play
        which havocs pleasures, processes of thought
          destroys, and tatters our design in matter
            till in dumb silence eyeless torment blinks.
              Yet – though in fleeting stars the fire shrinks,
                Though space expands, worlds burst, and frenzies shatter
          All our golden bubble with brute strivings bought,
            Yet shall I sing, while still this living clay
        Warms me, and lulls or thrills, my heart uplifting,
      Warms me, and cries to me, but warns that never
Till death is done will ebb the fatal dance.

12 June 1950

Another fishtail sonnet. The rhymes a to g are reversed in the second half of the poem, g to a. the two g lines with rhymes "blinks" and "shrinks" chime easily, but thereafter the rhymes get fainter and fainter, suggesting the running down of the universe. The remaining three fishtail sonnets follow.

Voice Remembered

Bamboos cascade to the river's edge like rain
  And glows with tawny gravel the jade stream.
   Now year on year flows back the waterfall,
     Flows to the fountain; fountains again your voice
       In the deep spring where leaping Pan scattered
        My dry heart's leaves. Yet still that fountain
          Fountains within. Comes back black Clodia's daughter
           Who tore my heart; nor hills nor healing water
            Availed to aid, nor dell nor dale nor mountain
           Made me forget, nor shock of legions shattered
          Where drunken kings with barbarous folk rejoice.
       I see them still, the empty centuries all
  With unknown faces thinning to a dream,
But still you summon me, your claws grown plain.

3 July 1961

*Written when I was working in Sarawak. It begins
with a typical Sarawak river bathing place. A river
brings water from the past to where you are
standing.   One might suggest that it brings scenes
from the past. Memory is like a fountain to the
mind. I put myself in the person of Valerius
Catullus. The Roman poet (b. 87 B.C.) whose love for
the evil Cloida is expressed in the poem "Keeping
Accounts", "Vivamus mea Lesbia atque amemus". I
then switched to the last years of the Roman Empire
in the west, when Roman princesses, like Chinese
princesses, were being used in the diplomatic game
to please the barbarians who were threatening
Rome and China at the opposite ends of the world.*

Cinder Buds

White in the tall air blooms the *force de frappe.*

Blue smoke flowers with spiralled roots of cinders,

And under mould the rock for ever slumbers.

Ours is a strength beyond the strength of numbers.

We build again with love from glowing embers.

Our shout is louder than the thunder-clap.

26 August 1968

Written in Douala on my arrival in Cameroun from Paris. I had been instructed by UNESCO to spend six weeks there studying French education, since my task in Cameroun was to help the two parts of Cameroun, the francophone and the Anglophone, to grow together. In Paris I had been somewhat mixed up with the students revolution, amusingly summarised as Liberte, Fraternite, Senilite. This poem was the first to be written in what later became the fish-tail style.

Spanish Spring

I woke in a forest of pillars in the middle of my years --

Gloomy this forest descending to end in hyena dark.

You came and glowed with the almond while ice still froze
on the pool,

Delight of Moorish kings.   Sudden within me flared

And flung fresh petals the rose. All around was song.

You and I   together were making a world in spring,

But words swept out from my ugly lips, unchecked. Scared

You heard the crackle of winter, looked at your desperate fool

Pelting stones at eyes on the fringe of the haunted park

And knew the bloom fading. Fell hot tears.

27 January 1974

*Written in Spain. This was a "fish-tail" poem, ten
lines, on the way to fish-tail sonnets. The mood is
that of King Bobadil after losing his kingdom to
the Spaniards.*

43

Mynah Bird

Voice of an Indian Bird in the street light,
   Lost in the street noise,
Do you sing to the dim-plumed people who pass,
Throb to the dawn rise of the arc lamp,
Thrill to the roar and rumble of buses' thunder,
Cowering under the cage bars?

                Come stars

Glinting over this jungle and tangle of ways,
Do you sing by the starlight of other ways and
jungles,
Noise-numbed voice of an Indian bird?

1939

I joined the army in September 1939, just before war broke out. On my 22ⁿᵈ birthday, 7ᵗʰ August, I took Peggy out to supper in an Indian Restaurant at the top of Tottenham Court Road where we were much spoken to by the Mynah bird.

44

Cotswold Skies

Over these wolds clouds go.
Brown fields dyed with an oxide
red, or with ram's blood drenched for fertility,
these I know.

Brown fields
surging with green spray, gay waves breaking
of young corn, I have known them of old,
so is hope born. And the lamp light,
with fire light, and warm stone
soothing the bone and flesh of us resting
at day's dusk, giving repose,
yes, I know these.

But who are those,
the unreposing, unrelenting,
tempest-torn, forlorn clouds ?

6 December 1940

My father-in-law had a farm in the Cotswolds. At the outbreak of war many fields were ploughed for the first time. They were all a rich red, but by the end of the war had become a rich brown due to many crops and much fertiliser. His fields were sited in an area of which a part had been cultivated since Neolithic times, near the Rollright stone circle. To my imagination his farm still had a strong Neolithic atmosphere.

London River

Tamed yet untamed river where tall cranes

Straddle the bank and nod to tugs

Busily churning upstream and down.

London town, risen from marshes,

Old fires burn in us yet,

Waking a flame, and new fevers.

London fret stirs like a wind in the reeds

through your streets. But I, when I watch your gulls

drifting seaward, think of lost voices

and cannot forget.

5 March 1941

Cormorant Flight

Tumbled cliff sprawls upon shorn crag,
Giant blocks torn from a time embedded
Deep in Devonian age, a rocky shore
Austere as world's grey dawning.
                                        Waters wash
And crash with their old unwearying crescendo,
Sevenfold repetition. The huge swell
Heaves out of ocean moonwards and relapses
As for a million ages.
                                Only the cormorant
Black as an omen of strife to come, races
And skims on and on, lonely into the night.

25 May 1942

Blackthorn

The sap is rising in the Blackthorn hedge.
Spring tingles at the root.
For all her maiden blossoming
She bears a bitter fruit.

14 April 1943

Asia

I in this land am small

And overcome with wonder.

Here plains extend over earth's rim,

Waters in thunder fall

From under hanging snow.

Below the path I see

The breathless river split

The reeling gorge asunder.

Mountains rise like giants

Brooding in cloudy castles,

And gods there are, Kanchanjanga,

Tien Shan -- the mountains of heaven . . .

Sadly my heart roves back

To stone-walled Cotswold fields

And the little lanes of Devon..

Spring 1945

See the comments on 'Asia' on the next page.

Comments on 'Asia'

Written when my course in Japanese in London at the School of Oriental Studies was drawing to a close. My prolonged reading about Asia was about to be confronted by reality. I felt it was better to write in anticipation than to wait till my impressions were dulled by reality, work and climate. I have never seen the Mountains of Heaven

India's Greeting

Heat holds all
In thrall
I walk the street
And a small voice whispers in my ear insane advice.
Beggars claim annas and pice.
Sweat flows.
Day goes
Crickets alone train
Their mad orchestra waiting for rain …
Then come clouds bounding across the sky
On a high wind. Far off I descry
A grey curtain. Palm trees shiver and sway,
Hawks scatter for cover. Down comes the rain.
Grass in a day
Turns poison green.
              Before my eyes
Fish and crabs materialise out of clay.
Round each mud-hole, yellow as mepacrine,
Frogs gather together, croaking loud, liking the weather.

****

Mountains like breasts thrust themselves up through the rain.
Gods possess the earth again!

1945

*Written shortly after arrival in India after the end
of the war.*

51

The Cost of Silk

Silk from the highest shelf in crimson folds
Falls on the counter-top. Fingers caress,
Eyes lighten. Here is wealth of emperors.
Now London's din grows less,
And dies away.

Camels plod slowly from some yesterday
Threading the singing dunes. Horizons hold
Promise of palms and threat of robbers. Still
The bales must quit the caravanserai,
Must seek the evening star above the hill.

Shadows rise up, Persepolis and Rome,
A fragrant whirl of gauze and gossamer,
Women at home
Or ---   withered at the mill,
The looms of Osaka and Manchester.

1945

*Probably towards the end of the year when I had
seen the silk shops of Bombay. There women bought
silk cloth by the yard, which I contrasted with what
could be bought by the Londoner's meagre coupons
in the 6th year of the war. This again contrasted
strikingly with the amply dressed and decorated
newly arrived U.S. troops and their families.*

Before The Rains

In this great land the clouds are high,
Boiling and black the troubled sky
Where birds sharp-eyed go slowly by.
    There is no sun.
But every blade of grass is brown,
Dust on the leaves, the earth burned dry;
From all things living comes a cry -
'Before another day is done
    Let rain come down.'

Now, when the earth is drained of light,
And fires are playing silver white
From cloud to cloud across the night
    Again, again . . .
As from some sponge in unseen hands
Small drops are formed; now in their flight
More drops and more to left and right
Are falling, and down comes the rain
    On tired lands.

24 Feb 1946

*Written after I had been in India for a few months.
I watched spell-bound the coming of the rain when
I was living near Bombay. Then I was sent up to
New Delhi where the weather conditions were quite
different. This poem was in Basic English which
seemed to suit the elemental conditions I had
observed in Bombay.*

53

Flowers of Bombay

The smell of *frangipane* billows up Malabar Hill.
Below in the twisted city exhausted people sleep
And some lie still.

At noon the *Flame of the Forest* startled the living with red.
Daily these flowers are scattered, where people daily weep
And burn their dead.

The rows of *Rusty Spearmen* tremble, the gates flung wide ..
Threshing of wings within where vultures for ivory strip,
Rip and divide.

Bombay 1946

Indian Dusk

The moon dies in the pale Indian sky.

Crows on house tops wake and gabble of dawn.

A man using a pump washes and spits.

Dogs bark. The Indian day has begun.

The sleeping city's sewers vomit and spawn:

Consumptives, lepers, things that creep on their hands

Whining for pity, pour in the maelstrom street,

The broken sons of a thousand heedless gods.

Black bats winnow the dusty air.

A witless driver thrashes his stumbling ox

Which shambles to midnight stall amid small fields,

And procreation plays its ignorant game.

Bombay 1946

Published in Isis, Cambridge 23ʳᵈ October 1946.

First Light in London

A thousand clocks say: Night is almost done.
A million bell-notes hammered out on high
say: Look! Green light is at last fingering the stars
      Under the morning sky.

26 August 1948

Late Night Final

The night is green. One lamp-like star
    Burns above old St Clement's shell,
    Fire blacked. What news do posters tell?
That night is green? That a lamp like star
    Pours its cold, delicious light
    On people hurrying home? The night
Is green, and yet one star may pour
    Thin poison in our ears, and say
    All kindness ended yesterday
In green of night, and envying stars
    See through the curtain of the sky
    The things we do. The world will die
When night is green. Then Lucifer
    Will ring with Hesperus no fair changes.
    No Hesperus, though the world arranges
Gay tomorrows, can defer
    The poison dawn when dusk is green
    And pours from heaven's eyes serene
On to our pages, near and far, the glitter of a venomed star.

1 October 1948

*St Clement Danes church was an empty shell for
some years as a result of enemy bombing, but has
now been repaired. I used to go home after work
from a bus stop very near this church, and gather
the thoughts which appear in the poem. The
nursery rhyme "The oranges and lemons says the
bells of St Clement's" refers, of course, to this church.*

Green Mountain

We came to Santubong, there saw many fishermen
Who stir the ocean's grey-green slime into little nets,
Refining lively ore; skeins hoisted in a thin wind
To dry, create distraught clouds. These laconically
Bellow from soundless mouths each dumb listless syllable
Against the mountain. Smoke, blue like the jacaranda,
Assaults in file the first tree-clothed precipitous chasms.
The hornbill calls and cries, cries, rasps from the very tops
Of those uncounted trees. High, far above her hover
Specks alien, fearful. Now slow circling the ultimate
Stub-pointing nose to thumb peak they vanish as - yes - as
Mist or as squalls that fall, drive, beating the attap thatch,
The steel and pewter seas' face beating to mercury
Till pearl and opal creams slide over the skin's ripples
And mask in pools the ooze where last hesitancies stop.

15 Feb. 1964

*This is an experimental poem written when I had
been in Sarawak for 8 years. I was interested at
that time in the possibilities of developing the
galliambic rhythm, where each line ends with 4
short syllables. Here I am trying out lines ending
with five short syllables - e.g. ". . . like the
jacaranda, " or "these laconically ...". Secondly I
was interested in the extent to which poetry is
affected by the local fauna and flora. A local
person reading this poem would find nothing
disturbing in its vocabulary. But one needs to be
familiar with the topography, zoology, etc. E.g. the
mountain has blue smoke creeping up its side "in
file" i.e. a narrow snake of smoke, because a
pathway has been cut in the mountain side which
acts rather like a chimney.*

Boat Fever

I must go down to the mud again, to the reeds with their
rotting pith,
And all I ask is an old boat, and a rope to pull her with;
And a valve to clean and a plug to change, with grey beards
shaking,
And grey sweat on grey face, and a grey dawn breaking.

I must go down to the creeks again, for the call of the ebbing tide
Is a top priority urgent call that may not be denied.
And all I ask is a rainy day with the landass pouring,
A crash and a sound of rending wood, and my best friend snoring.

I must go down to the bar again, to the gay bohemian life,
For the wife's away and the boss is away, an end to trouble
and strife.
And all I ask is a merry yarn from a laughing fellow rover.
He can laugh on the other side of his face. The damned
trip's over!

Date uncertain but early 1960s.

*Written in Kuching for Jim Warburton & his yacht,
to commemorate the stepping of the Mast of a tall
ship in the Sarawak River, with due respect to the
author of "Sea Fever".*

Mount Cameroon

My clay clogged feet must climb again
 By woodland paths and tortured waters.
I must get up above the rain,
Break through the clouds and find the sun.
 This work is done. I long to wander
High among the golden grass.
I wish to see the lost days pass
 like shadows creeping from their cupboards.
I must climb up above the grass
 where cold winds shrill in climbing spirals,
where twists the blue convolvulus
 no longer, but the strong hawk circles
endlessly above the rocks.
 I must go on past lonely places
  where mocking echoes
  rack the boulders.
I shall climb up by unused stairs,
  see shapes ascending
  and descending,
  welcome lost voices,
  unknown faces,
   future and past
   in turmoil blending,
  and lose myself
   among the
   stars.

18 December 1969, Buea, Cameroon.

Home-coming (1)

The waves drive in and smash with a boom of thunder
Hard on the sea-wall, drench with spray like a shellburst
Cars and buses that pass. Crows wheel in the wind
And snatch at the palms, while the old Arabian Sea
Churns its mud like Tiber or Yellow River.
   When did the first dhow race pepper-heavy for Egypt,
Or Hangchow junks slide in with celadon ware?
Did chanting wretches cram the stinking holds
With snowy cottons? Did other men sweat and starve,
As now, that princes might dine with abandon, flaunting
Their women in hungry eyes, or listening to music
That wails and ebbs on the night air, leaving a jetsam
Of ineffectual memories tinged with self-pity?
   Who cares? The stokers strip. Gangways are up,
And one more vessel bucks through the scudding foam.
An opal softness begins to lighten the skies.
White gulls, stout -boned, quit rocks and guide us home.

22 June 1972

*Vividly recalling my departure from Bombay 26
years before when I was on my way home after
seven years of war service in the army.*

*Many things have changed since then. Bombay has
changed its name. Men are no longer employed as
stokers, since diesel engines have replaced the
furnaces for steam turbines, whose heat caused the
men to strip. Every evening they used to gather on
deck at sunset, and having established the
direction of Mecca, would pray together.*

Home-coming (2)

Gladly I make for this secret place
patterned with ivy, dappled with umber
and shadow. Relax. This is home. It is home.

Men here once hacked rock, but elder
quickly shaded the shattered face
of earth. Rough grass and campion grew
white and pink, with the tall cow-parsley.
Slim trees leapt to the light and threw
their branches across. They daily comb
and brush their leafy twigs and needles.
Far below new trees grow sparsely.
Now I am glad. This is home. It is home.

I will go in as I used to go
lifting the beech trees' green portcullis,
but sudden a jay shouts "Passport ! Passport !
Here is an alien. Watch ! Mind out !"
A thousand others begin to shout
of danger, foreigners, police, controls --
and I stand numb, my mind distraught.
I reek of petrol. I creak with plastic.
Synthetic bathroom odour rolls
from my unclean skin. With inelastic
step I fall, to alarm reagent.
An owl patrolling to and fro
Observes me a blundering secret agent.

22 June 1972

*On returning home one always felt like a foreigner,
because the home country had changed so much
and often very rapidly. I was struck also by the
different emphasis which different countries put on
things which require wealth or at least money.*

Fete Galante

You swept towards me like a swift in flight,
Then passed, and driving upward, onward, up,
Pointing your toes toward the evening light
You froze an instant and fell back. My cup –
How full!
               But then I saw your smile harden
As up you soared again. Now the spring light
Was fading.   Now time stops.   I wait far under
The whirl of petticoats …..
                          Soon in our garden
The mob, the crash of unexpected thunder.

4 March 1998

Written on visiting the Wallace Collection with Angela.

63

Sleeping on Deck

About this steady mast stars frolic and reel.

I alone constant watch the gyrations of the universe.

Everything flows they say: gaseous seas, solid rock

Stretched by each passing star with rainbow stress.

Oncoming waves are sundered. One by one

Each generation's ripples wash what shores

Or heave and sink in the lake of infinite motion?

Thoughts flow backward and forth, westward, east;

India, crippled giant reaching for light;

England, green isle hidden in mind's mist.

Everything flows. Homeward our ship goes.

September 1946

Comments on 'Sleeping on Deck'

I was given a berth on a Liberty Ship horribly overcrowded with troops going home. My two-berth cabin was occupied by four officers beside myself. I made my bed on the floor. This cabin was adjoining part of the refrigeration system. Before we set off it developed a leak with a foul smell for our benefit. Visitors to this cabin were instantly sick while they stood in the doorway making enquiries. I had taken to my bed before we started for fear that someone else might occupy the space. I found that while I was lying down I was OK, but was sick the moment I sat up. A friend who was sleeping on deck found me on the third day of sailing, and persuaded me without difficulty to make my bed next to his on deck. The monsoon was blowing and the sea off Bombay was exceedingly rough. After about a week it improved as we drew near to Africa and proceeded up towards the Red Sea. (See also Homecoming 1 and 2.)

The Quiet Square

In this quiet square the leaves are turning

Green to yellow, brown to black;

On Sunday, clocks will be put back

In this quiet square where leaves are turning.

Back go the hands but not the hours

To my cold fingers, long dead flowers

In this quiet square where leaves are turning.

Page after page in history's book

The half-regretted smile, the look

Of this quiet square where leaves are turning;;

And still red lips, brown arms I see

Folding and falling back. The tree

Is shaking its summer gold for burning

In this quiet square where leaves are turning.

4 Oct 1948

Fall

Rainfall, waterfall, leaf-fall, snowfall.
    The long years changing green and grey.
My heart is sadder than the woods' black branches
    Waving the last summer days away.

1938

Villanelle (II)

Softly sounding like a bell
      Line on line there come to me
Verses of a Villanelle.

But as a summer roses' smell
      Louder makes the winging bee
Go from flower bell to bell,

So does every parallel
      Make me other verses see
For another Villanelle.

Then in fields of asphodel
      Let my winging thoughts go free
Go from flower bell to bell,

Go from rose to Philomel,
      Moonlight song and cypress-tree
To the end of Villanelle.

Quiet then! It is not well.
      Let the verses ended be.
Give us now the deep-tongued bell
For the death of Villanelle.

13 May 1938

September

The cart has cleared the last upland sheaves
and bordering elms droop yellow leaves.
An urchin bat in the clear sky weaves,
  and the low moon hangs on the wane.

The cuckoo has foisted his fatherhood
and the weary dove has reared her brood.
An ancient stillness possesses the wood.
  The autumn has fallen again.

The poem describes a form of farming which has disappeared. (Cart, sheaves of corn, elm trees). I worked on the farm of Mr A B Harvey, my future father in law at Great Rollright, Oxon, for a few weeks before joining the BEF, (British Expeditionary Force), in France in late autumn, 1939.

Breath of Summer

Give me the smell of ivy; give me bees;
      And summer flowers, and give me summer sun.
Give me the skies of Greece, the full leaved trees,
      And the sad light of day when day is done.
Give me the forms of men and women walking,
      The running rivers, and the waterfall,
With falling rain; at sundown old men talking
      Of other days gone by with summer's all.

18 March 1940

A poem in Basic English, to be read slowly. I was having a week's home leave from my battery on the outskirts of Lille. It had been a bitterly cold winter, followed by a savage form of 'flu. At that time I used to send poems to magazines, hoping they would be published, but with no success. So when at home in Oxfordshire I wrote a letter to Robertson-Scott, the editor of The Countryman, asking for his advice, and enclosing two poems, of which Breath of Summer was one. He replied very soon saying he liked them very much and had sent them off to friends of his who were editors of magazines. In due course they were both published. I assumed from this that it is not really the quality of the poem which matters, but the reputation of the sender. The phoney war came to an end on the night of May 9th. My poem Campaign 1940 explains why I was too busy after that!

To Anaesthesia

They dragged me out to my martyrdom,
Out of the silent hall of pain.
"Why do you lead me thus?" I cried
To the woman in white on either side.
"In the cause of science", they all replied
And the car moved forward again.

The great high priest was dressed in white.
And on either side was a satellite.
I was the victim of that rite.
I the lamb to be slain.

Slowly the dancing maidens come,
Back and forth to a beating drum,
Louder my ears and temples thrum
Wilder the surge of the brain.

Why do you lead me forth from the light
Into the empty fields of night?
'The ways of science are just and right
Thou art the beast to be slain.

Now in a circle round they go,
Round in a circle moving slow.
Shall I be flung to the shades below,
Or swept to the realms of delight?

See in his hand the cruel blade
Priest of god, may your hand be stayed.
"For the cause of science the feast is made"
He comes! He comes! It is night,
Black, black blacker than the night.

Before an operation, classical delirium. KR

*This was probably written in 1941 after a motorcycle
accident incurred as an officer dispatch rider. AR*

The Meeting

I had a meeting yesterday
    With one I'd never seen before.
Only one sentence did she say,
    But I shall hear it evermore.
In our vast drab metropolis
    She seemed a stranger for her eyes
    Reflected lights of brighter skies,
Though dark as willow pools.

                And this
Was strange, that being loved by men
    She still was fair, was loving still.
    I saw her and my blood ran chill.
She smiled and looked upon me then.
These words she whispered and was gone.
    "You were my love in Babylon".

16 Feb 1942

Sorbiodunum

From this hill fort I survey
The giant works of yesterday.
Sweeping acres drowse and sleep
Beneath the frowning of this keep.
Faintly mottled on the downs
Slumber Neolithic towns.
And when sunset spills its red
Across these ancient English skies
The barrows silhouetted rise
Where crouch the long forgotten dead.

Old men, distressed with plagues and fears,
We in our time are sick at heart.
No pause is ours nor magic art
To ease us through our tale of years.
Yet with our hands we wield the things
Which drag philosophy from kings.

20 Feb. 1943

Spring

The almond tree was flowering yesterday,

A thousand stars dropping in the rain.

Brown are those leaves, dead now;

And I am old again.

Undated, but written by Lt. K.G. Robinson, C.D. Experimental Station, Porton, Nr. Salisbury, Wiltshire. The original had the word "little" between "those" and "leaves" but the poet crossed it out. I would have thought it helped the rhythm, but Robinson always defended his poems quite fiercely against editorial interference! L.H.J.

Seven Seas

I have seen seas more blue than morning dream

And waves breaking silver in the convoy's slipstream.

I have seen phosphorous fires wink after dark,

And slink through jade green water the questing shark.

Shall I yet cross the wastes of fog and frost,

Reach in the end the kingdom of the lost,

And find that lonely ocean where my heart is tossed?

Published in "Oxford Magazine", Dec 1946.

Fortune of Soldiers

When I was three and twenty

The world was all of rose;

The hot-lipped guns beneath the stars

Sang havoc through the night.

Now claiming no surrender

But seeking heart's repose,

I find your arms unused to war

Put my resolve to flight!

1947

Written in Leyden to amuse a friend

Full Circle

I crouch beside the fire glow

And think of seven years ago.

Gaily we pitched the barley sheaves

Though Poland fell, though fell the leaves

And France went down and London burned ….

    Now the grinding wheel has turned

Past Volga, Don and Danube; past

The Channel and The Rhine. At last

Grown sick of hope, the lamp burned low,

I think of seven years ago.

14 Feb. 1947

This poem shows signs of the same reaction to the war that I wrote about in my note following Invitation to Dance, (next page).

Invitation to Dance

Build it up with wood and clay
      (Dance o'er my Lady Lee)
The debris has been cleared away
      To make a city fair to see.
Under the ruck of rubble and stones
      Centuries deep are skulls and bones.

Babylon had four high walls
      (Dance o'er my Lady Lee)
Lots of fun when evening falls,
      just the place for you and me.
Plenty of laughter, plenty of hate.
Someone comes by the water-gate.

Lovely music in Singapore
      (Dance o'er my Lady Lee)
The Japs have only reached Johore.
      Why the rush to get to sea?
Everyone says it'll be all right.
Goodnight ladies, goodnight, goodnight.

* * * * * *

The world we built is broken down
      (Dance o'er my Lady Lee)
Wolves in packs have come to town
      And hungry people rise and flee.
Kings and Councils have had their day.
Children are left in rags to play.

11 March 1947

Comments on Invitation to Dance

The first three verses may be read in a light and mocking voice, but the last one must be read absolutely seriously like a dead-march. In it, Lady Lee has been transformed from the gay lady who frequents doomed cities to the grim and terrible spirit of Nemesis who now bestrides the whole world.

For people in England 1947 was a time of mental depression, for the war was over, and everyone had expected things to get better quite quickly, yet in many ways they got worse. When some money had been accumulated and we thought it would go on re-construction, Churchill shot off with it to Greece one Christmas morning, and used it to prevent the Communist faction getting control of Athens, after which the Russians would have got control of the Eastern Mediterranean. Well spent, no doubt. It was particularly galling to have French friends call on us at home, and tell us with delight about the marvellous new docks being built on the French coast with international money, far better than the battered old docks at Southampton!

I don't think anyone knows who Lady Lee was. Apparently some sort of witch character who visited doomed cities. The Oxford Dictionary of Nursery Rhymes, O.U.P. 1951, PP.270 - 6 , gives many versions of this old song derived from the primitive fear of large rivers. I imagine that Xerxes, King of Persia, thrashed the Hellespont in BC 480 to make his army understand that he was more powerful than any river. When a new bridge was being built the usual precaution for its safety was for a living person to be built into its foundations. (Cont.)

Sometimes it was a little boy who became the watchman, and would be given a candle and a piece of bread to have with him. He would then be bricked in to die. " London Bridge itself is not without a tainted reputation, for there was a tradition in the capital that the stones of this great bridge were once bespattered with the blood of little children." In 1872 when the Hoogly Bridge was being built across the Ganges it was feared that to placate the river each structure would have to be founded on a layer of children's skulls. Even as recently as 1959 in Malaya the Pahang State Engineer had to make a public denial that the State wanted seven human heads for the construction of a new bridge, and for that matter when the Public Works Dept. in Sibu, Sarawak, was building a new bridge, why was Robinson from the Education Dept. spending so much time talking to the P.W.D.?

Mortal Comfort

I in this tumbling world of spindrift pitched
rock with the cauldron's eddies, stare bewitched
at whirlpools clutching straws, count life enriched
if I survive, and, when no frenzy mars
the mounting horror, see with grim delight
lean walls of water racing through the night
whose crenulated phosphorescent light
mocks the blind tumult of a million dying stars.

Sometimes deep in the hollow mirror of my brain
faces like mist condense, form flesh and burn
with lips of poppy red that bid me drink
and so forget. Then would I gladly turn
to your dear arms, and lose myself, nor shrink
from future grief, though tears must fall like rain.

17 July 1947

I was well into the subject matter of my thesis and
drawing on ideas and phrases from the Tao Te
Ching. One of these is used here in the lines:
Sometimes deep in the hollow mirror of my brain
Faces like mist condense
The "lean walls of water racing through the night"
seems to anticipate the tsunami which caused such
destruction in Indonesia in 2005.

81

Waste

Wasted the years when love was strong,
    Wasted the days when clouds went by
    White-sailed, snow-topped; when hope was high,
And flowered summer nights were long.

Wasted the fish in seas put back,
    Wasted the grain from other lands,
    Wasted the work of other hands,
Wasted the yellow, brown and black.

Wasted the very earth which goes
    Through unused Space, unpurposing,
    Year in, year out, while Fall and Spring
Make birth and death from rain and snows.

Still on it goes, past star and sun,
To the Great Nothing, Man's day done.

Undated, but written at Heath Farm, Great Rollright. An uncharacteristically desolate poem, and only included to show that even the sunniest of characters can occasionally hit rock bottom. L.H.J.

The Singer Within

This music still my shattered senses stuns.
Still smell I blood in Arcady, or serve
Thessalian rites. Time catches up, nor swerves
Nor speed can save those who before Him, Karma-ridden run.
Under the moon upon those hills in Thrace
The ivy crown, the drumming and the dances
Burn through my sense. For aeons yet no chance
To drink the waters of forgetfulness, when he who chases
Down the dim ways sees with renewed delight
His devotee reborn for yet another
Savage exaltation. Though the weird word severs
And breaks in spray to light a thousand mothers'
Faces in their fruitfulness, yet ever
I must be strung and racked for music on unholy nights.

See the comments on 'The Singer Within' on the next page.

Comments on 'The Singer Within'

This sonnet deliberately breaks the rules. Instead of 8 lines then a break followed by 6, it has the break after the first 4 lines, followed by 10 lines of increasing tension to the last line which has 7 beats in it, whereas all previous lines have fairly normal iambic pentameters, except the fourth which like the last line has 7.

This almost certainly belongs to the time when I was back in Oxford after the war, 1947 - 51, and picking up the threads of the old classics for the Pythagoran scale, later to be found as a Chinese scale. I was interested in why some people write poetry. The Greeks said that it happened when one of the muses touched the poet with her finger. I have sometimes felt this.

The main point of this poem is that poetry seems to be plantlike in some people and comes up unbidden again and again as if marked out for some religious sacrifice.

(See foreword LHJ.)

Their Infinite Variety

Women there are who return from ages past,
   waking my heart as once on vast plains
    horses thundered, umber, chestnut and black.

Women there are whose hair is fair as the light,
   elfin fine, floating when autumn sighs
   and dies by starlight in woods of silver birch.

Women there are whose skin is pale and cold,
   but a hot wine runs beneath, spreads and suffuses
   a glow of the northern sun in frosty waters.

Women there are whose bodies are tawny gold.
   They drink the sun at noon, and wait, and hunger,
   haunting the hours when shadows a-hunting go.

Women there are who come like a dream and pass,
   whose eyes can speak of silence beyond all telling.
   They shrive my heart, and stir me like withered grass,
    and leave me, an empty dwelling.

1 July 1949

Revised 4th April 2002.

85

Selva Oscura

We walk alone in a grey mist: no unveiling
Of sun through clouds, but only a faint gold
Breaking on shafts of silver. The slow wailing
Grows and fails of pines in the forest; their old
Tales half-told decay, through centuries tossed,
And lonely we make our slow way, lost.

Yet in the night when clouds ride foul
And cumber the air, to strike with brown light
The mountain ridges; when bat and wild owl
Hide and cover, nor dare to take their flight
Around the sky's boundaries, suddenly thunder
Will smite with a loud chime all towns asunder,
And, through a rent beyond the delectable mountains
The sky lifts and the light of a city fountains.

28 December 1950

After thoughts about the war. The slow wailing (of sirens), but the sky lifts. Selva Oscura (dark woods) is how Dante introduces his views of life.

Blind Justice

Still this great earth, of iron and granite made,
Tears through the stars, and swings about the sun.
Still the frail crocus and the green washed larch
Foretell a myriad springs to come, or tell but one.
In India now the vivid trees proclaim
May's horror. Those thin folk must bear their dust
Till clouds at last release their far off rain
And churn to gold the fields of unjust men and just.
Northwards the ice-packs break, the frozen rivers
Roar where the salmon leap again from sea.
In hungry lands men clamour to be filled.
Cities still belch their poison; ancient wrongs
Cry out for justice; fields are yet untilled;
And blind men, praising blindness, fumble to be free.

9 April 1947

*This poem was selected to be one of those
representing Oxford verse in 1952. It was read by
Ludovic Kennedy and later broadcast by the BBC.*

Bitter Song

Wash up, wash up the rancid cups.
Scrape out the gravy from the spoon.
Who would have guessed that maggots bred
From many a golden honeymoon?

Wash out the years and days and hours
When life was breathless, love was long;
Forget the whisperings and the song.
Heap on the bonfire faded flowers.

Yet from my cloud-hung cataract
There pours a stream to wash the soul
And rinse away stale love and hate.
I from that shining stream extract
Love in a land where no bells toll
And slams like a guillotine the gate.

26 Sept 1961

Slow Beat

My slow heart beats its seasons round.
    The springing pulse, the failing year
Fall and revive. Silence and sound
        Leap to my ear.

Failures returning in success
    Breed bitter victories, to succeed
Recurring chains of emptiness
        Filling our need.

Dear woman, giver of dark bread,
    For whom alone rank love and fear
Were stirred and stilled, like wheat waves red
        At ebb of year,

Together we had merriment
    Till candles guttered, and no less
Beneath the crumbling pediment
        The Graces bless

Others like us whose seasons round
    Will chase the pulsing tumbling year,
Till they in snow on the fire wheel bound
        Know you most dear.

22 November 1967

Great Rollright. I have often noticed that a poem, while it is pouring itself onto the page, has a terrific interplay of words, so many that when the writing is done many of them evaporate and many of the secondary meanings disappear. I thought it would be interesting, when one is still hot from the writing, to get some of this down in prose. Only minutes after Slow Beat was finished therefore, I wrote five paragraphs to this effect, which are attached. (Cont.)

Further comments on 'Slow Beat' written immediately after completing it: -

My heart beating slowly now seems to beat more slowly as it has told its tale of returning seasons. My life is like an estate in time, and my heart beats its bounds against encroachment. In the springtime of life we have a leaping pulse. When we get old it fails. Our life has a spring and autumn just as the year does. But within one life there are many little springs and autumns as our interests flare up and die away again. All our living is a succession of alternations typified by silence and sound. Each in its turn has a striking impact.

Failures in general, and people who are considered to be failures in particular, sometimes come back to their point of origin, and at their return bring success with them, or are successful at the second attempt. But when they are successful, success does not necessarily taste sweet. Victory for one person is bitterness for another, and this bitterness can be handed on to succeeding generations like a blood feud, so that when one looks back on past series of strife and victories, they stretch out like chains to bind us, and they keep binding us anew, bringing no real joy but an emptiness of soul. Victories temporarily fill our needs, but a Taoist emptiness is really what fills it.

Where then do we turn for stability in this shifting emptiness? To Woman who gives us the primitive food of mankind, like the bread and wine of the Mother Goddess. Her bread is dark because it is associated with dark caverns under the hills and midnight ceremonies, and in its dark colour there is a suggestion of blood, as there is in the redness of wheat. Ultimately it was for woman alone, whether

90

goddess, mother or wife, that our most violent emotions were stirred, emotions that spring up like rank weeds among the wheat in primitive fields. Like the surface of the ocean they were subject to silence and sound, ebb and flow, changing from green to red and back again as dawn and sunset, spring and autumn followed one another.

I myself have had joyful days with my loved woman, ignoring time till reminded by the guttering of the candles. Now I realise that time has been passing, that whole civilisations have perished, but even after a civilisation has gone, a graciousness lingers, which blesses those people who are aware of it.

These people too will have their hour when the pulse beats fast and time seems to stand still, until at last their waning year comes tumbling down, like Jack and Jill, just as "flowers betumble the chestnut spikes" and later the leaves fall. At last they too, with snow white hair, in snow white clothing like victims for sacrifice at dead of winter, will be laid upon the great flaming wheel of the world that circles among the flaming stars, and will be no less happy than the Stoic on the rack in their understanding that Love is over and under all.

Adieu aux mysteres

Little love, so much you gave me -- your courage and
warm affection and tumbling hair.

I shall feel you for ever near, in the dark mind's crater,
crouching there,

Waiting for me to say what I always left unspoken,
always thinking

Of others who were and are, and who cannot be forsaken.
Then I recall

The pool of Vaucluse, the troubled water. You drank from the
Sichar well,

Spoke to the dauphin, boldly riding alone with sceptre and orb
in a fiat.

Is Pax true peace?   ---   Fiat orbis

Et urbis pax --- it was you who gave me bread and wine
and fishes leaping

Silver in a copper pan. Now all is ended. Now
with outstretched arms

I bless you as once you blessed the ragged corpses three
on jagged crosses

As we swept out through the green and lemon skies one dusk,
not seen again.

Then you looked up and saw bright Venus beckon me,
sweet Magdalen.

The Shrinking Circle

My eyes unscrew from tropic suns.
    Colours leap out where all was dim.
    Across these Berkshire hills a theme
Twists through the centuries and returns.

Up from the chalk a green mist springs
    Where once the folk hoed endless furrows.
    Stark on the skyline loom the barrows
That housed the hopes of unknown kings.

Two pigeons pass with wings that beat
    Fast as the racing years have flashed
    Alternate night and day, since Rome spread
Panic ripples from marching feet.

There, where the patient Saxons dug
    Ditches to drain their water meadows,
    Mallard within the bulrush shadows
Still persist, nor can forget

The menace and the shrinking circle
    Of unsubdued and sovereign land.
    Reactors breed their alien kind
Looping the world with hostile girdles.

9 April 1973

Written in Cameroon.

December in Cologne

Two inflexible fingers of God point
   Gnarled in stone bones fire-blackened.
   The Rhine, ringing with wars, sour and sickened,
Drives like troops in column of route to the front.

      Come little lass, these airy spires
        Make homes for doves. In windy places
        Crows look down on smiling faces.
      Here we may listen to distant choirs.

But still they tramp, the marching feet, and north
   And east they bang and blister into the cold,
   Where the dry snow-stinging winds snatched and yelled
At legions born, recruited in the south.

      Your hands are hot, your step is light.
        Forget the wars. Ignore that spire.
        A man roasts chestnuts on the fire.
      Here let us shelter from the night.

Yet can I not forget the endless river,
   Grey lips that cry, partings and tears and pain.
   Eastward the wind-swept never-ending plain
That leads to China. Soon we must part forever.

Dear love, we cannot be together;
   You must seek the Hellenic south
   And I the north. We are not free
To dally in the summer weather.
   You are my lost Eurydice.

23 Dec. 1975

94

Comments on 'December in Cologne'

When I was returning to England for Christmas, after 7 years with UNESCO in Cameroon. I had routed my return via Cologne because I was anxious to see the famous museum of this ancient Roman colony. It had essentially been a place of meeting and parting. I am imagining here a Roman soldier going the next day to the northern Rhine defences. I suggest that verse 4 would be spoken by the girl, but this is quite optional. I think of verses 2, 4, and 6 as being like a Greek chorus offering a different point of view.

Alternatives

Seated alone in my cave I think this thought:
I must scratch out a message for future men --
If any are left -- in words few, simple and short.

Flower days gone. City streets
Bent and burnt among lakes of dark glass.
Hillocks of brick. Bushes starting to sprout.
Land ridges and furrowed by black rain.
Once there was music here. A stark plain
Now harks to the wind's whistling. Alone
I watch spring and summer give fruitless birth.
Rats, no longer meek, inherit the earth.

The last gods vanished in shrill pain.
Lao Tzu warned us, long ages ago,
That the Tao is not unkind, nor yet kind.
Still it is there, endless, beginningless, so.
It blends the Yang and Yin, the hard and soft,
In countless constellations, and even though
In a million worlds Love may bloom in vain,
In a million more it will die and be born again.

25 December 1982

*Written while spending Christmas with my son
James at Brill. See footnote to Villanelle for
Angela, and quote from Feynman. I sent a copy of
it to Ludovic Kennedy, see Blind Justice (page 87),
who said the poetry was all right, but it is a very
hackneyed theme!*

96

Thrush Song

See how they come, sweet thrushes on the lawn,
  and sing of other thrushes on their lawn
    from dawn till dusk.
Breathe in, breathe in the scent of myrrh and musk
  From dawn till dusk, the garden scent I love;
then cease. Enough ! Storms overwhelm me, whelm me,
  strike with lightning eyes through every room,
  sweep me forth, a leaf in the whirlwind, spent.
And I return, dawn after dusk after dawn
  to quiet gardens which tell of simple things,
  lawn and thrushes and dawn and spent musk.

1 June 1990

*My wife Peggy died suddenly at the end of
September, 1987. I often sat in our garden in
Comberton, reflecting quietly on life. This is where
I wrote this poem. The whirlwind in line 8 suggests
the arrival of visitors!*

Generation Gap

When I was a little boy
I wore flint knives in my belt,
Tattooed my face with berries,
Kept a feather in my hair.
Early, much too early,
I was sent away to school,
Froze the upper lip
And learnt to cry inwardly.

Now grown men
Walk about in lace and feathers,
Wear a single earring,
Dance and love with abandon.

Gladly would I join you,
Brave generation,
But my upper lip is frozen.
I have learnt to cry inwardly.

2001

*Written early in the new millennium. See the
reference to this poem in the foreword. ALR*

On the Way Out

There comes a time to say goodbye for ever,
When words stick, smiles are creased and memories flood
Past all repressing. Now, beyond our guessing,
The future opens -- or is shut. Now never
Again will blow cool winds or pulse hot blood
At unexpected meeting or caressing.

   Wait! Who comes here? Gaunt monsters out of sleep.
They nod with swaying necks, they smile at me!
And there go I, small boy with bandaged knee,
Towing a kite, while you alone wade deep,
Searching for baby ducks without a mother.

   Now the great monsters turn, they bark and howl
Wailing like bombs seconds before they strike,
Yet me they have not hit.
                    The monsters change
To Chinese dragons, winged with golden leather.

They bear me up past storms and violent weather
To where the Earth shines small and blue and strange.
The dragons melt away. Onwards I drift
Through the soft sift of stars, a flowing river,
And without oar or sail, I drift, drift on for ever.

13 Feb. 2002

Consolation

So many years we loved in quietness.
    Now looms ahead a city in the dusk.
    Low-walled it is, and fragrant. Rose and musk
Gently perfume the air that heals distress.

And yet years slowly gathering in the dark
    Alarm and stir with mounting tide of fears.
    What are these cries and why this fall of tears?
This is the land where shadows loom most stark.

Bring back the light. Bring songs in magic rune.
    Sing of the days gone by – the red and green.
    Now let us glow with glories that have been,
And find no clouded sun, nor dimmed the moon.

29 December 2004

Written when KR came out of hospital and was very ill. A.R.

Elegy for an Unwanted Child

The poisoned city sobs and stirs,
    Its life blood pumped down concrete ways.
Here bindweeds challenge stunted firs
    To mark the slag of ugly days.
Etiolated lives persist
    In cage and corridor and funnel.
    When evening falls, the crowded tunnel
Spills furtive couples keeping tryst.

Yet on this pool the nenuphar
    Floats lovely lamps within the black.
        Children are born and born again.
    This child, his light unloved, sank back
Into the murk. Would I could hear
    His small voice singing in the rain.

The End

Dust and drums and drums and dust –

   It comes. It comes.

Mortal longings decay and rust.

     Sad chords waken. Each fresh clash strums.

Old wounds half healed break through the crust

And vultures come.

Now naught remains of youth and joy,

High hopes are withered, stale perfumes cloy

And all is fused in dull alloy

    Where worlds are dumb.

Keeping Accounts

Let's make the most of it, Lesbia, let's make love,
And the unkind words of older, bitterer persons
Take at the value of less than a half brass farthing.
Suns may go down, yes, down and up again,
But for us when once is gone our day's short light
It is night unending, one and made for sleeping.
Give me a thousand kisses, then a hundred,
Then a thousand again, then a second hundred,
Then still another thousand, and then a hundred.
Then when we've made it come to thousands and thousands
Let's put the point in the wrong place, keeping the answer
Secret even from us, and from green-eyed persons
Green at the thought of there being such numbers of kisses.

Vivamus, mea Lesbia, atque amamus,
Rumoresque senum severiorum
Omnes unius aestimemus assis.
Soles occidere et redire possunt:
Nobis cum semel occidit brevis lux,
Nox est perpetua, una dormienda.
Da mi basia mille, deinde centum,
Dein mille altera, dein secunda centum,
Deinde usque ad altera mille, deinde centum
Dein, cum milia multa fecerimus
Conturbabimus illa, ne sciamus,
Aut ne quis malus invidere possit,
Cum tantum sciat esse basiorum.

Translated 2 July 1939

See the comments on 'Keeping Accounts' on the next page.

103

Comments on 'Keeping Account'

Catullus, Valerius, was born in BC 87 in or near
Verona and died about 47 BC. He was about
twenty years older than Horace, and like Horace
experimented with metres not previously used in
Latin verse. He also introduced from the Gaullis
language the word kiss, in modern French baiser.

Far Away

Sweet one, when you were here, the house was full of flowers.
Sweet one, now you are gone. . . cold is my bed.
The silk cloth on our bed is rolled up. No sleep for me.
Three years it is, but the breath of your being is with me still.
The sweet of your body is blowing round me forever,
But you my love will never come again . . .
Sad my thoughts like yellow leaves falling down.
Green grasses are wet with the morning rain.

3 Dec 1941

*I have translated this poem which was written by Li
T'ai-Po, (Li Bai), who lived in the 8th century, into
Basic English. Like our William Cowper he had
hoped to be selected for a quiet post in government
service, but was not chosen. Like Cowper he spent
his life in pleasant company writing poetry, but Li
Bai lived in a large boat and travelled up and
down north China visiting friends. When he said
goodbye he gave them as a present one of his
exquisite poems, noted for their moving simplicity.
After his death his friends gathered them up and
preserved them for posterity.*

Further comments on 'Far Away'

In translating Chinese poetry there must always be
a loss which cannot be replaced. There is the simple
meaning of words, but many of these carry an
aura of further meaning which is probably
different in the two languages. There is
onomatopoeia in both languages, which enables
the poet to heighten the effect of the words he has
chosen, but the effect of the words may well differ
because each language uses sounds special to itself.
As written Chinese does not spell words out with
letters, but uses symbols to suggest meanings,
Chinese uses on occasion what might be called
"pictotopoea", arranging characters containing
pictorial symbols which strengthen the atmosphere
of the poem through the eye as onomatopoeia does
through the ear. So a poem describing life in the
mountains might be rich in characters which
contain a radical element such as 'water',
'mountain', 'vapour', 'grasses', 'trees' and so on. In
addition there is another device which cannot be
used in English because Chinese is a tonal
language and English is not. In a tonal language
the words are pronounced to a tune, such as we use
in English to distinguish a question from a
command and other subtleties of expression. But
in Chinese the whole poem may be set to a tune
consisting of rising and falling notes, and
sometimes a famous poem with a good tonal
foundation may be imitated in later poems.

The Sailor

A soft wind under a blue sky.
He sees the lighthouse through the shipcords going;
Then Egypt gone. No cloud over low cloud blowing.
In his brass plated ship his heart is high.

He will not see the harbour side again.
In wastes of sand down on the green sea floor
The mountain waves will keep him evermore.
Through twisted trees the wind sends word of pain.

There in deepest fold of moving sand
Where comes no star, no moon, no change of light,
Let him at last have an untroubled sleep.
And to his bones washed to the Grecian land
May earth and water give a sailor's right –
No weight upon him, earth. No noise the deep.

22 September 1941

Translated from "Le Naufrage" of Jose Maria de Heredia.

To Passchendaele

To Passchendaele! To Passchendaele!
The order comes. The march is set.
The leaves are green. The grass is wet.
Then let us go to Passchendaele.

To Passchendaele! To Passchendaele!
But will they send their sword, their sons
A second time, and man the guns
And drum the drums of Passchendaele ?

               Across the sky the white clouds sail
And heaven is blue. Why, not again
Must we obey the brain-stormed brain
That sends his guns to Passchendaele?

To Passchendaele! To Passchendaele,
Where gunners fell, where horses fail,
And over all things sings the flail
Of lead that lashes Passchendaele.

So let God crumble, seraphs quail,
Let strong and ugly things rejoice.
Sometimes we faintly hear the voice
Of women float o'er Passchendaele.

December 1939

*The first world war battle where Jack Kipling died.
Kenneth especially loved Kipling's stories and
poems. One of our favourites was The Glory of the
Garden. My Son Jack, was one of the last plays we
saw together. AR.*

Before Louvain

Twilight is falling in the whispering beechwood.

No letters from home. A sickness runs

Through village and farm, as the armies draw near.

Rockets shatter the night, and a man's voice cries:

"To your guns! To your guns!"

This describes an alert about the night of the 15th May 1940 as the German army closed on the French border town of Louvain, which was held by the British 3rd Division under General Montgomery. I was with the field artillery. We had occupied a convent from which the nuns had withdrawn previously, marching in file like soldiers, each carrying a small amount of baggage. See Campaign 1940 (next page).

(The original was written in the little notebook KR carried with him during the war. - AR)

Campaign 1940

Springtime came with a flush of flowers
Lacing with pink the orchard way.
   The whole earth trembled with marching powers,
And April melted into May.

   May awoke from golden dreaming,
Woke with a scream before morning light;
   Then day by day came people streaming
Down from the north and east in flight.

   Onward the armies sped, as ever
The country folk came trudging back,
   Homes foregone, and resting never,
"Ces avions font trac-rac-rac."

   High in Louvain the convent clock
Slowly docks each crawling hour.
Mother of God, come down in power!
   The buildings rock and sway and rock.

   Sudden withdrawal. Night occupation.
Village inn. Beer gone flat.
   Bleating kid on railway station.
That's our road, and that, and that.

   Joy we have now from tepid water.
Trees overhead, how fair to see!
   Daylight fails. The guns' mad laughter
Withers the shadows. They gather and flee.

   The glad sun mocks, for the spring is hollow.
Kindly folk are no longer free.
   Column by column the units follow
Happy to reach the spattered sea.

To reach a sea in violent motion
Churning the slaughter with bomb-wave wild.
On the dark sands' edge a sailor rots,
  Rocked as a child by his mother Ocean.

1940

After action; when the jumble of impressions had sorted itself out. I distinctly remember a trench 8 feet deep dug across a road by the local people to stop German tanks. Then they had placed above it a gigantic saw on which were written the words: 'Pour scier les couilles d'Hitler'!

In a Hospital Garden

Now it is frail November. With small steps
Like a child I feel my way to the garden's roses,
Lift their sick heads and smell them. Not here emerges
breath of ether or death. My heart leaps
At the faint flush in the rose's heart, like golden
Mornings of August in our great summer, when I
In speed and strength rejoiced, and sped down byways
Of England, or muted watched the high clouds unfolding
grim lanes of airmen.
                              The rose dies,
Petals unheeded fall to earth. Through a funnel
of grey days the memory swift recedes
Of sunlight, brown faces, tables for two,
Numb partings, sweat, sandbags, curses,
The sharp road at evening, shock, and the tunnel.

November 1940

*I was a dispatch rider for Montgomery taking a
vital message and driving very fast. The accident
described took place on 18th September 1940 when
I failed to make a sharp turn on my motor-bike
and spent four months in Cosham Hospital,. The
petals unheeded falling to earth are pilots in the
Battle of Britain coming down by parachute, if
they were lucky.*

The Ultimatum

Bombed cat of bombed house
    Sits alone, but unperturbed.
Though nightly blitzes do their worst
    Bombed cat is undisturbed.

Scornful of evacuation
    Still he sits where he has sat.
No screaming bomb or doodle bug
    Have dethroned bombed cat.

Undisputed lord and master
    Still he stalks his primitive way.
His hunting grounds are unaffected,
    And as plentiful the prey.

This is bombed cat's declaration
    "When you all have had your say,
Send the Reich <u>my</u> ultimatum –
    Here I am and here I stay"

10 May 1941

Altered in 1945 after the use of the "V bombs".
(These were flying bombs, the V standing for
Vergeltungswaffe - reprisal weapon, the Doodle Bug
being the VI).

113

Farewell

Now I must say farewell to my domain,
No more at evening with naked feet
To thread my way toward the ample river.
I shall rise up and climb that hill again
No more, nor sleep drunk on your starry wine
But keep my sad heart safe in brine of tears
Unnumbered years.

19 March 1944

Written on waking at 1.00 a.m. Sunday:
'Due to go to the Eastern Theatre of war fairly soon.'

(The only time when the poet seemed undecided!
L.H.J.)

Thoughts of War In A Cotswold Churchyard

Within these upland acres
   Ten peaceful hamlets lie.
    Still thrilling to the skies
     Mounts up the singing lark.
If copper moon should wake her
   No hesitant reply
    She makes, but after moonlight dies
     Endures a transient dark.

We too that empyrean
   Have made to chant by night,
    With grim repeated flights
     Have rocked the world with thunder.
Not yet is raised the paean
   Nor passed the plague which blights
    Our earth-born faith, the ancient right
     Of those who lie there under.

1944

*See the comments on 'Thoughts of War In A
Cotswold Churchyard' on the next page.*

Comments on 'Thoughts of War In A Cotswold Churchyard'

While learning Japanese in London I would spend any days of leave I had on my father-in-law's farm in Oxfordshire not far from the great air base at Moreton in the Marsh, caricatured by the Home service as Much Binding in the Marsh. While there I often heard preparations for the great thousand bomber raids on Germany. At dusk they would begin to take off, singly or in small groups, with perfect timing and engines perfectly tuned. After a short time the whole sky began to ring as if a metal cover were reflecting the sound. All night they were about their business, and then at dawn they began to return, some with a healthy roar, but some stuttering or with an engine cutting out. Sometimes, if a plane was returning with a bomb on board, if its remaining engine cut out, there was a momentary silence followed by the sinister sound of an explosion. Soon after dawn Joe the milkman would come pedalling up from Moreton to milk our cows, and would shout the news all around the farm: "Another 1000 bomber raid last night. They were swilling out the cockpits with hoses like they was butchers' shops."

Thoughts Among the Rubber Trees

A spring spills over by the temple steps.
When evening falls they hear the song of thrushes.
Not here! When Teramoto's spirit sings
Blood gushes.

The crow clamped fast upon his blackened tree
Natters of rain. In cloud the sun is setting.
Kuroki chats of torture, slashings, loot
And bayoneting.

Sakuramoto – cherry brook in spring.
Dainty white waves flash silver round the cape.
When "Horse-teeth" gets a whiff of violet scent
It's murder, rape.

1945

See the comments on ' Thoughts Among the Rubber
Trees' on the next page.

Comments on 'Thoughts Among the Rubber Trees'

This poem was written in the year we landed in Singapore to take over from the Japanese after their surrender, a word they did not care to use, preferring to say Senso no ato-de; "after the war". I cannot give an exact date. It would probably have been about Christmas, by which time I had learned of the barbarities of the Japanese towards Chinese civilians even more than to our Prisoners of War. The screams of people being tortured in the YMCA at night led people returning home late after work to prefer a longer route. One of the striking things about the military Japanese was the way that some of them combined a highly developed aesthetic sense with a lack of feeling for the victims of war. Many Japanese officers combined a love of poetry or painting with ruthless efficiency in their military calling. I was sent to a post near Kluang in northern Jahore, where we were screening Japanese POWs in the hope of identifying those who had been responsible for atrocities on the Burma-Siam railway. The interrogating team lived on a rubber estate; hence the title of this poem. Sakuramoto means "Cherry spray". "Horse Teeth" is an example of the unflattering nicknames often given to the Japanese officers by the civilians.

Thoughts in Kensington Gardens

Snow fallen by night, white, unfreckled with soot.
The absurd horse Physical Energy sags, its naked
Rider mantled with snow, manly torso and knees.
    In Germany now they burn, butcher and freeze.

30 January 1945

*The statue of Physical Energy seemed during the
war to represent all the things, such as strength
through joy, which Hitler had recommended to the
German people. By 1945 the Nazi virtues were
reaping their own reward.*

Occupation

Gone is the leaping hate which sent my blood
Coursing and boiling with the spite of war.
A cold dismay and semi-guilt creeps in
Where righteous anger hotly flamed before.
Three little boys, dead quiet, hand in hand,
Watch him, their father, bleeding on the floor.

17 January 1946

One of my many recurring thoughts, memories and nightmares of war.

Thoughts for Monday

Zero hour approaches. I review my leave
and wait for the week's assault, its earnest rhythm,
unfelt politenesses, shutting of doors and books.

  Sometimes I flee the world for a windy garden
in the springtime of myself -- oh, the mad fluting,
and see the moon riding high over the almond,
hear the market gossip of rooks in elm-tree villages,
and pick again my first chestnut candles.
Now it is Monday. Unmagic magic casements!
Close the door, my love, upon all putrefaction.
Your voice was low and lovely, and still I love you,
love you as in the noonday of our English summer
when Death sauntered carelessly among the couples,
and the grim executioner stalked our battlements.

21 January 1948

*This was one of the poems written about the war in
retrospect. By 1948 I was in my second year at
Oxford having a second bite at the cherry. This
had been made possible by the Chinese Government
which gave three scholarships for spreading an
understanding of Chinese civilisation, one each to
Oxford, Cambridge and London. I was given the
one for Oxford.*

Epitaph

When I am dead will the wise Alchemist
Look up my mortal record, note, and file me
    "Conformed to type. Insignificant variation."?

So, alas, my little individuality
Will cease like the last spark in a grey fire;
My ever restless hubbub of hopes and emotions
Will fade right out; at last the plastic molecule
And surging atom will be poured once more in the
crucible
Of the giant laboratory.

        One hope! Let me be eccentric,
Have a progeny of monsters, be incurably, amusingly insane.
Then may the Alchemist concede this touching epitaph:
    "Finally a most interesting experiment".

20 January 1941

Published in Oxford magazine Cherwell, 19ᵗʰ August 1949.

Top of the House

			glow,
		low her a	reddening
	The stairs	are steep;	she sees be-
Renelle	reborn	a Dracu-	line.
			stair,
		daughter, she	climbs the
	Each night	reborn -	a devil's
The stairs	are steep.	The night is	green.
			air.
		flutter in the	evening
	Each night	she climbs,	where pigeons
Each night	she climbs	the winding	stair.

a vertical
tunnel a
shaft
to
Renelle
in
INCENDIE

15 May, 1968

Written in Paris. Note— start at the bottom of the stairs and climb up, then, tumble down to…

Peace Old Soldier

Once a prisoner-of-war,
Now home from Singapore –
A mere five stone.
Those nurses nursed him back to vigour,
And made of him once more
A handsome manly figure.

He was a carpenter by trade
Yet found his life hard to restore;
The prison years, the scourge of war
Left nightmares which refused to fade.
In solitude he'd sit and think,
No succour came when it was needed.
He found his only friend was drink.
Then in a bedsit, all alone
He'd listen for the telephone,
And fantasise about his life,
About lost friends, lost sons, his wife,
The love that needs no other link.
Inside his flat the walls were bare
No paintings, pictures, hanging there;
No treasured keepsakes from the past
Of halcyon days that could not last.
And yet inside each tiny flat
The resident would tell you that
Mementoes of his skill and care
Are in abundance everywhere.
No task too trivial, none too tough,
The best alone was good enough.
His acts of kindness here and there
Became his only epitaph.

Final request from Kenneth.

A Short Biography of Kenneth Girdwood Robinson.

"Second son, born 5am at St Mary's Nursing home, Parsons Green." - so reads the entry in a tiny leather diary dated August 7th 1917. The diary belonged, according to family folklore, to a direct descendant of Robert Bane of Invervak, Harold Robinson a London lawyer, this son was Kenneth.

The family lived in Pinner, but Kenneth's father soon decided to move his young family, out of what was then a smog laden London, to Tunbridge Wells in Kent. He spent most of his childhood in the area before entering Wrekin College, Shropshire in 1931.

We met in Cambridge in 1990. A love of poetry, nature, the joy and pathos of music, were just some of the things that gave us such affinity. We believed together we could find that "quiet place that's green away from all mankind." There was however literary work planned or to be completed first.

Work at the Needham Institute on *Science and Civilisation in China* with his friend of fifty years, Joseph Needham, already over ninety, was a priority. He was also anxious to get his ideas for a very special book that had formulated in his mind into print. The poetry he had been writing since he was a boy still scattered in numerous notebooks, on scraps of paper, and some clearly lost, needed collating. There were indeed many projects to complete for a man already approaching the autumn of life.

This short biography is intended only to present Kenneth the literary man, the writer, the poet. His personal life so rich with happiness, sadness, stories of adventure, fun and accomplishment, military memoirs, and tales of Sarawak, must wait for another time.

Having had a fascination for poetry from an early age, by the time he began to read Classics at Oxford in 1936 he was already a published poet and had received prizes not only for his own work but also for his poetry translation.

In his second year, while studying Greats at University College, he was approached by C.K.Ogden, the inventor of 'Basic English' who requested that Kenneth write some poetry in 'Basic'; some of those poems can be found in this collection.

While still at Wrekin College in Shropshire his essay on Sir Stamford Raffles -which won the first prize of fifty guineas, a fortune to a schoolboy in the 1930s - prompted the head of the Raffles family to engage in correspondence with this young lad, correspondence which still survives, suggesting that he consider a career in Malaya. He did in fact work in Japanese translation and interrogation centres in Malaya, New Delhi and Singapore in 1945-46.

Kenneth was commissioned into the Royal Artillery and in December 1939 he joined the British expeditionary force in France as a gunner officer. The campaign in the Low Countries followed in 1940 and you will recognise many poems written during these desperate times, including his experiences at Dunkirk.

Hospitalised in 1942 in Cosham following injury he was visited not only by General Montgomery his commanding officer but by his friend C.K. Ogden resulting in Kenneth collaborating with H.G.Wells, at Wells' request, to translate the much celebrated *Time Machine* into Basic English. The vision was that people with a limited command of English could not only read and enjoy this imaginative and important work, but that Basic English could also open many other doors in education and literature.

126

Selected by the War Office to learn Japanese, he met John Pike who was to become a lifelong friend. Both were seconded to the Intelligence Corps and it was in this capacity that Kenneth served in Malaya and New Delhi as translator and interrogator. Later when interrogating the Japanese in Singapore he was present for the release of his own cousin from the dreaded prisoner of war camp, Changi.

During this period, poems of a sombre nature spilled from his pen on to scores of little scraps of paper. Due to the constraints of war and its obvious literary limitations, sadly some only survived in part. Grief for friends lost and horrors witnessed certainly coloured that period of Kenneth's writing.

After the war he worked for a short time on the preparation of educational booklets, filmstrips, etc., and on language simplification and research with C.K.Ogden.

In 1946 he returned as Edwin Arnold Memorial Scholar to Oxford, to study Classical Chinese. His plan was to become an archaeologist working at the Western end of the Great Wall of China. It was here in Oxford that Kenneth met Dr Joseph Needham and agreed to write a contribution on acoustics for one of the volumes of *Science and Civilisation in China.*

Apart from bringing up a family, studying and writing a thesis, he found time to write new poems some of which were printed in *Poetry from Oxford*, and the freshly re-introduced *Oxford Poetry*, which after four years silenced by the war, is a marvellous document for historians of poetry.

These post war years were not years of plenty and sadly it was not easy to find a suitable place to live particularly if you had a small child. For a while Kenneth lived with his first wife Peggy and young son James in a real gipsy caravan in Oxfordshire, sold later for twenty guineas, a princely sum to them at that time. The small family embraced the essence of this extended community life style and I believe there are elements of that influence in his book, *The Way and The Wilderness.*

In 1949 Kenneth set up the Makers Club, the aim of which was to bring together writers of verse and music. Activities included the reading of verse and plays, singing, speech, rhythm and ultimately the recording of examples of polyphonic verse. Sadly it has not been practical to include any of his polyphonic poetry in this collection, but some is still available, together with some old 78-rpm records from his Makers Club days, to anyone interested.

In 1952 he joined the Overseas Education Service and was appointed Education Officer in Singapore where he initiated the first teacher training in the Chinese language. Some especially happy times in Sarawak, ultimately as Director of Education, followed where he not only made many wonderful friends but wrote short stories of his experiences. In Sarawak he would often frequent the villages and Long Houses of the Dayaks and other peoples, their remarkable orchestras evoking in him the music of the Choe and Han. The fourth volume of *Science and Civilisation in China* was published while he was there and included Kenneth's contribution, the section on Acoustics, combining not only his interest in, but his knowledge of, sinology, music and Chinese history.

In 1968 he joined UNESCO as advisor to the Government of West Cameroon on educational planning in order to help them integrate education in the Francophone and Anglophone parts of the country. During this period he wrote a number of books and papers on education and some of his poetry in a lighter vein comes from the years spent in South East Asia.

Kenneth was a fine man who typified all that was best about a generation whose plans, lives and education were interrupted by the war in which they fought, a generation that had to mature abruptly. His long career in education continued in Paris and Hamburg still working for UNESCO Institute for Education as editor of the *International Review of Education* and other publications until 1979, when he decided it was time to join his old friend Joseph Needham in Cambridge as sub editor of *Science and Civilisation in China*. Together they worked towards the opening of The Needham

Research Institute and library, a welcome move from their cold, cramped offices in Brooklands Avenue.

It was in Cambridge that Kenneth achieved his long held ambition to write a book about the complexities of modern science and the challenges that result from our present understanding of the universe. *The Way in the Wilderness* was published in 1993, followed by its sequel, *Beyond the Wilderness*. Both books were greatly influenced by his Taoist ideas and principles. His friend of 50 years, Joseph Needham, died March 1995 at the age of 94. *Joseph Needham: A Soliloquy*, written by Kenneth and used at Joseph's memorial, was printed in the *Cambridge Review 1995*.

Kenneth's editing of the final volume of '*Science and Civilisation in China*, Volume 7 - Joseph's conclusions', was a mammoth task and he was becoming increasingly frail. However, never one to disappoint, he managed to complete the work and it was published by the Cambridge University Press in 2005 and launched at the University Library Bookshop just before Christmas of that year.

Kenneth sadly died soon after, in June 2006, before he was able to complete his other lifetime ambition to assemble just some of the many poems he wrote into a small anthology. This is the result; poems inspired by Peggy his first wife, poems of a little son who died in infancy, poems of other lands, other dimensions, and the stark poetry of war. Poems too that are very special to me.

In one of the many letters he left me, addressed, 'to Angela in the darkest hour', he asked me to: "Sort out my poems and in sorting them we will be talking together."

I hope you enjoy our book.

Angela Robinson.

A Tiny Snapshot Of History

The author of this poetry collection, Kenneth Girdwood Robinson as a new undergraduate at University College, Oxford, 1936

"How does it fly, Mister? – a question for Kenneth at Oxford University Gliding Club's opening meeting

Kenneth at War
(the serious side of 1944)

A week after returning from
action at Dunkirk Kenneth
marries Peggy in Great
Rollright Church,
June 1940

The joy of Cameroon, handing over more supplies for the rope bridge. 1963

Sharing a meal with friends of 50 years,
Lu Gwei-Djen and Joseph Needham

Punting on the river Cam with granddaughter, Lottie

Kenneth the academic preparing for the launch of Volume 7
of Science and Civilization in China, in 2005

Kenneth at John O'Groats

Kenneth with grandchildren, John, David & Laura,
at Audley End

Making friends in Egypt

And Suffolk

Far from the madding crowd

A family celebration of Kenneth's 80th Birthday
at son James' house in Feock, Cornwall.
Delia (daughter-in-law), Sophie and Charlotte
(granddaughters), with Kenneth and Angela

Kenneth and Angela outside Ditchburn Place,
Cambridge, after their wedding, June 1991

Kenneth in the autumn of his years

Index

Printed in the United Kingdom
by Lightning Source UK Ltd.
135713UK00001B/86/P